ASHE Higher Education Report: Volume 43, Number 3
Kelly Ward, Lisa E. Wolf-Wendel, Series Editors

Campus Unions: Organized Faculty and Graduate Students in U.S. Higher Education

Timothy Reese Cain

Campus Unions: Organized Faculty and Graduate Students in U.S. Higher Education
Timothy Reese Cain
ASHE Higher Education Report: Volume 43, Number 3
Series Editors: Kelly Ward, Lisa E. Wolf-Wendel

ASHE HIGHER EDUCATION REPORT, (Print ISSN: 1551-6970; Online ISSN: 1554-6306), is published quarterly by Wiley Subscription Services, Inc., a Wiley Company, 111 River St., Hoboken, NJ 07030-5774 USA.
Postmaster: Send all address changes to *ASHE HIGHER EDUCATION REPORT*, John Wiley & Sons Inc., C/O The Sheridan Press, PO Box 465 Hanover, PA 17331 USA.

Information for subscribers
ASHE HIGHER EDUCATION REPORT is published in 6 issues per year. Institutional subscription prices for 2017 are:
Print & Online: US$477 (US), US$557 (Canada & Mexico), US$626 (Rest of World), €406 (Europe), £323 (UK). Prices are exclusive of tax. Asia Pacific GST, Canadian GST/HST and European VAT will be applied at the appropriate rates. For more information on current tax rates, please go to www.wileyonlinelibrary.com/tax-vat. The price includes online access to the current and all online back-files to January 1st 2013, where available. For other pricing options, including access information and terms and conditions, please visit www.wileyonlinelibrary.com/access.

Delivery Terms and Legal Title
Where the subscription price includes print issues and delivery is to the recipient's address, delivery terms are **Delivered at Place (DAP)**; the recipient is responsible for paying any import duty or taxes. Title to all issues transfers FOB our shipping point, freight prepaid. We will endeavor to fulfil claims for missing or damaged copies within six months of publication, within our reasonable discretion and subject to availability.

Back issues: Single issues from current and recent volumes are available at the current single issue price from cs-journals@wiley.com.

Disclaimer
The Publisher and Editors cannot be held responsible for errors or any consequences arising from the use of information contained in this journal; the views and opinions expressed do not necessarily reflect those of the Publisher and Editors, neither does the publication of advertisements constitute any endorsement by the Publisher and Editors of the products advertised.

Publisher: ASHE HIGHER EDUCATION REPORT is published by Wiley Periodicals, Inc., 350 Main St., Malden, MA 02148-5020.

Journal Customer Services: For ordering information, claims and any enquiry concerning your journal subscription please go to www.wileycustomerhelp.com/ask or contact your nearest office.
Americas: Email: cs-journals@wiley.com; Tel: +1 781 388 8598 or +1 800 835 6770 (toll free in the USA & Canada).
Europe, Middle East and Africa: Email: cs-journals@wiley.com; Tel: +44 (0) 1865 778315.
Asia Pacific: Email: cs-journals@wiley.com; Tel: +65 6511 8000.
Japan: For Japanese speaking support, Email: cs-japan@wiley.com.
Visit our Online Customer Help available in 7 languages at www.wileycustomerhelp.com/ask

Production Editor: Abha Mehta (email: abmehta@wiley.com).

Wiley's Corporate Citizenship initiative seeks to address the environmental, social, economic, and ethical challenges faced in our business and which are important to our diverse stakeholder groups. Since launching the initiative, we have focused on sharing our content with those in need, enhancing community philanthropy, reducing our carbon impact, creating global guidelines and best practices for paper use, establishing a vendor code of ethics and engaging our colleagues and other stakeholders in our efforts. Follow our progress at www.wiley.com/go/citizenship

View this journal online at wileyonlinelibrary.com/journal/aehe

Wiley is a founding member of the UN-backed HINARI, AGORA, and OARE initiatives. They are now collectively known as Research4Life, making online scientific content available free or at nominal cost to researchers in developing countries. Please visit Wiley's Content Access - Corporate Citizenship site: http://www.wiley.com/WileyCDA/Section/id-390082.html

Printed in the USA by The Sheridan Group.

Address for Editorial Correspondence: Coeditors-in -chief, Kelly Ward, Lisa E. Wolf-Wendel, ASHE HIGHER EDUCATION REPORT, Email lwolf@ku.edu and kaward@wsu.edu

Abstracting and Indexing Services
The Journal is indexed by Academic Search Alumni Edition (EBSCO Publishing); Education Index/Abstracts (EBSCO Publishing); ERIC: Educational Resources Information Center (CSC); Higher Education Abstracts (Claremont Graduate University); IBR & IBZ: International Bibliography of Periodical Literature (KG Saur).

Cover design: Wiley
Cover Images: ©

For submission instructions, subscription and all other information visit:
wileyonlinelibrary.com/journal/aehe

Advisory Board

The ASHE Higher Education Report Series is sponsored by the Association for the Study of Higher Education (ASHE), which provides an editorial advisory board of ASHE members.

Contents

Executive Summary

THE UNIONIZATION OF instructional workers is a central feature of U.S. higher education, with more than a quarter of those teaching college classes covered by collectively bargained contracts. Though dated, the best existing numbers indicate that more than 430,000 faculty members, graduate students, and related personnel are in bargaining units; thousands more are in nonbargaining units affiliated with organized labor. As recent events in Wisconsin, Indiana, Iowa, and elsewhere have demonstrated, faculty unions are also controversial and subject to attack. Opponents question the need for faculty unions and claim that they lead to inefficiencies, inhibit needed flexibility, and operate in opposition to both traditional notions of professionalism and ideals of shared governance. Some further attack them on purely political lines. Proponents counter that, among other benefits, unions bolster professional status, provide faculty with a needed voice in governance, and help increase salaries in a sector that has often relied on poorly paid instructors. Graduate student unions are even more contested as stakeholders disagree about whether student status supersedes instructional roles and precludes employee status. Too often, conversations about and arguments regarding faculty unions take place in the absence of research evidence. Just as problematic, many considerations ignore the existence of unions of instructional workers.

This monograph examines the existing research literature on the attitudes about and effects of faculty and graduate student unions. In so doing, it highlights the great scholarly interest in the topic in the early years of widespread bargaining but the increasing neglect as the growth of faculty unions slowed after the Supreme Court of the United States' decision in *National Labor Relations Board* v. *Yeshiva University* (1980), which severely limited the abilities of tenure-line faculty at private colleges and universities to collectively bargain. This neglect is especially unfortunate as the broader changes in U.S. higher education and its staffing, as well as the methodological advances of recent decades, might offer new or different information about this key aspect of higher education organization and policy. Still, useful research does exist and helps shed light on the causes and effects of unionization both historically and in the modern era. Capturing, analyzing, and synthesizing this research is the main purpose of this monograph.

Following an introduction to key issues, this monograph begins with a brief overview of the history and context of unionizing in higher education. Now nearly a century old, the unionization of college faculty began in late 1918, when a small group at Howard University affiliated with the American Federation of Teachers (AFT) in hopes of improving their conditions and influence while also securing additional federal funds for the institution. The Howard local was soon joined by those at other institutions but only one survived for more than a few years. The 1930s saw renewed interest in the AFT although most faculty did not unionize and many viewed it as antithetical to the professional status they sought. By the late-1940s, faculty unionization had suffered significant setbacks, but in a handful of cases union locals experienced success, including negotiated contracts at Howard, Fisk University, and Tri-State College. Widespread bargaining began to take hold in the 1960s, fundamentally changing the nature of faculty unionization; at a number of institutions it changed the conditions of faculty work. The American Association of University Professors (AAUP) and National Education Association (NEA) joined the AFT as national organizations vying for collective bargaining units, and by 1980, a quarter of faculty were organized, many at community and regional colleges. In the aftermath of the *Yeshiva* decision, the spread of bargaining slowed significantly but by the turn of the century graduate students increasingly turned to unions to improve their working conditions. In the years since, their efforts have continued and been joined by the significant push for non-tenure-line faculty to unionize in their own bargaining units, including the Service Employees International Union's (SEIU) drive to organize on citywide bases.

After addressing this history and describing the larger modern trends—unionization is more prevalent in public than private institutions and at those that emphasize teaching more than those that emphasize research, for example—this monograph turns to the research on the effects on unionization, taking into account how it has changed over almost five decades. It begins with an area that dominated the research on faculty unionization in the early years of bargaining: faculty attitudes and voting behaviors. Early studies pointed to demographic characteristics including age and gender as being related to support for unionization, although as methods advanced similar findings were less prevalent. Looking across studies, level of compensation, general political and union attitudes, views on faculty influence on governance, satisfaction, perceptions of union instrumentality, and having a peer network that is in favor of unionizing generally appear to be related to support for bargaining.

Numerous studies have addressed the effects of unionization, including dozens that have considered various aspects of compensation. Early studies that matched unionized and nonunionized institutions largely found short-term union wage premiums but diminished returns in later years, though many lacked consideration of cost of living or other important factors. More recent research using large-scale data has raised questions about whether premiums continue to exist at 4-year colleges and have suggested that they are smaller at 2-year colleges than previously believed. Evidence regarding whether wage distribution is different at unionized and nonunionized institutions is inconsistent, though some evidence of the continuation of existing distributions exists. There is also some evidence that unionization is linked to greater pay equity, although it does not come close to overcoming gender wage gaps. Finally, several studies have also found that unionized faculty are more satisfied with their salaries than nonunionized faculty, though more work needs to be done.

Among the most significant concerns of opponents to unionization are the effects it might have on governance, including potentially shifting authority away from existing senates or encroaching on issues traditionally under their purview. Although some senates have been negatively affected—even abolished—and the overall shifts in power are unclear, much research associates collective bargaining with gains in faculty influence. Where strong senates had existed, they retained authority; where they did not, unions provided new ways to provide faculty voice. The existing research further points to union effectiveness in establishing formalized tenure and grievance procedures, but little success in providing robust protections against retrenchment.

Some research has explored issues of collegiality and climate, highlighting that organizing campaigns can be divisive but also providing counterexamples where they were not. Studies of administrators' attitudes toward bargaining have emphasized negative experiences but questions remain over how widespread such views are. Some have suggested that studies considering only the views of those at the bargaining table necessarily find conflict and dissatisfaction that the broader faculty and administration do not experience. Moreover, a negative climate is associated with the decision to unionize, raising questions of causality even when such a climate exists. Similar questions are implicated in the research on satisfaction. The research is fairly consistent that unionized faculty are not globally more satisfied than nonunionized faculty and may be less so, but whether that is because of, a cause of, or unrelated to unionization is less clear. At the same time, there is some evidence that unionized faculty may be more satisfied with certain aspects of their jobs, such as compensation, but less satisfied with others. Some scholarship has focused on other potential effects of unionization although it has failed to offer definitive understandings. The few studies that have explored institutional effectiveness, for example, have offered little clarity on its relationship to unionization.

The unionization of non-tenure-line faculty and graduate students has begun to receive attention in recent years, largely in the form of insider perspectives and individual case studies. Early work on part-time and non-tenure-line faculty in larger bargaining units was conflicted, as some found that benefits accrued to workers in these categories whereas others found those at the highest and senior ranks gained most from unions. The limited recent research on non-tenure-line faculty offers evidence of substantial gains for unionized faculty in areas including compensation, security, and status, with only some concerns about potential loss of flexibility. Graduate students in unions have reported that they believe their unionization has resulted in important gains in wages and protections, although the actual research is sparse. Importantly, however, despite widespread fears that unionization would damage student–faculty relationships, research is consistent that it does not; in some situations it has improved them.

These and the other findings detailed in the monograph point to much more research-based knowledge about unionization in higher education than might be presumed considering how rarely it is brought into broader conversations in the field. At the same time, much more work needs to be done. The bulk of the research was undertaken decades ago in a different context and with methods that would be considered basic in the modern era. Since the end of the National Study of Postsecondary Faculty in 2004, true national studies have been difficult to undertake necessitating that most understandings are based on limited samples, usually from one or a few institutions. Additionally, research has suggested that the outcomes might differ not just by institution but by sector, yet the implications have not been fully addressed in the literature. For example, despite the fact the unionization is more prevalent at 2-year than 4-year institutions, most work focuses on the latter. Additionally, more non-tenure-line than tenure-line faculty are unionized, but most research focuses on the latter or considers all faculty regardless of employment status. As such, though substantial research exists, much more is needed to fully assess the impacts of unionization on faculty, institutions, and higher education as a whole.

Foreword

RECENTLY, RESIDENT ADVISORS at a small private college sought the right to form a union. Doctoral students serving as graduate teaching assistants have also sought the right to unionize as have adjunct and non-tenure-track faculty, faculty at community colleges, and other faculty groups at both public and private 4-year institutions. Underlying these decisions to unionize lie issues of faculty career trajectories, overworked graduate students, work–life balance issues, and increased demands on faculty. These issues have been frequently cited as important concerns about higher education in the academic as well as popular press. Despite these headlines, the role of unions in shaping faculty and graduate student life, as well as the role they play in establishing relationships between faculty, emerging faculty, and administrators in higher education, has been somewhat overlooked. This is in spite of the fact that close to a half million faculty members work in unionized environments. Why they are overlooked is uncertain; perhaps it is a function of the general decline in union participation throughout the country or perhaps it is a by-product of more managerial environments in higher education, where shared governance is compromised. Regardless of the reasons of the lack of attention to unions, the topic remains important given the role that unions play in negotiating contracts, supporting fair work environments, and maintaining the principles of shared governance. Understanding the research-based perspectives on the role of unions in higher education is more important than ever.

In this monograph, *Campus Unions: Organized Faculty and Graduate Students in U.S. Higher Education,* author Tim Cain provides a comprehensive review of the literature related to all aspects of faculty and graduate student unions. The monograph includes a history of unions and the context in which they were established and have evolved. Further, the monograph points to the nuances associated with unions for graduate students and faculty, as well as the important roles unions have played in creating workplace structures that support faculty and graduate students. Looking at the research collectively sheds interesting and important light on unions, but perhaps more important, about the relationship of unions to important milestones in the history of academic life. For example, Cain's review of the literature highlights the roles that unions have played in supporting academic freedom and shared governance. The findings from the analysis and synthesis related to unions are also interesting because existing research looks at relationships between faculty satisfaction, collegiality, and attitudes as correlates to unions.

The monograph is also timely in that it addresses topics associated with non-tenure-track and part-time faculty as well as graduate students—topics that are integral to any conversation related to contemporary academic life given the important roles these individuals play in carrying out central research, teaching, and service functions. The emergence of unions for contingent faculty and graduate students has highlighted the complexity and totality of what these groups do to fulfill the mission of U.S. higher education. The monograph is a great companion piece to other monographs in the series, for example, the monograph on contingent faculty published by Kezar and Sam (2010), the monograph on faculty careers and work life published by O'Meara and her colleagues (2008), and the forthcoming monograph by Alleman and colleagues (in press) on collegiality and non-tenure-track faculty. Although these monographs do not focus on unions per se, when read in tandem with Cain's work they highlight the roles that unions play in shaping faculty work life and realities.

The monograph is sure to be of interest to those who study topics related to collective bargaining and unions and other faculty-related topics. Those who study history will also find relevant the thorough historical coverage in the monograph. This monograph will be of interest to faculty senate leaders, deans, provosts, and others with responsibilities related to faculty in unionized environments. As researchers of faculty-related topics, we learned from reading this monograph about the important and overlooked roles of unions in multiple aspects related to faculty life and we think you will as well.

Kelly Ward
Lisa Wolf-Wendel

Acknowledgments

I WOULD LIKE TO thank my graduate student and faculty colleagues from the University of Georgia, the University of Illinois, and the broader Association for the Study of Higher Education and History of Education Society communities who have humored, supported, and encouraged my thinking and talking about unionization in U.S. higher education. Philip Wilkinson and Danielle Kerr, especially, provided greatly appreciated assistance with this work. I would also like to thank Adrianna Kezar for her encouragement to undertake this monograph and Lisa Wolf-Wendel and Kelly Ward for their support, guidance, and editorial suggestions.

Introduction

IN LATE MAY 2016, the administration of Notre Dame de Namur University formally recognized Service Employees International Union (SEIU) Local 1021 as the agent for its entire faculty, becoming one of only a handful of private institutions in the 21st century to agree to collectively bargain with a union including tenure-line faculty (Flaherty, 2016b). One month later, the City University of New York (CUNY) and the Professional Staff Congress (American Federation of Teachers Local 2334) tentatively agreed to a new contract that will provide 10.41% salary increases to the faculty over a 7-year period, much of it retroactively, as well as health insurance and increased security for adjunct faculty members. The local's overwhelming ratification of it at the beginning of August ended more than 6 years of contractual struggles in a period of economic austerity, although it left some concerned that more was not gained for adjuncts (Schmidt, 2016; Zamudio-Suaréz, 2016). The next day, August 4, faculty at Tallahassee Community College voted to affiliate with the United Faculty of Florida (UFF), becoming the faculty of the 26th institution to be represented by the union (Dobson, 2016). Concurrently, graduate students at private universities across the nation prepared their own organizing efforts, hopeful that the National Labor Relations Board (NLRB) would overturn earlier precedents and grant them the right to bargain with their institutions (Trottman & Belkin, 2016). On August 23, those hopes were met when the NLRB ruled that graduate students working in teaching and research roles had employee relationships with their universities, and thus, had the legally protected right to unionize (*Columbia University*, 364 NLRB 90). Each of these events in the summer of 2016, and numerous similar situations both before and since, points to a key but often neglected characteristic of U.S. higher education: the widespread unionization of its instructional staff.

Almost two decades ago, Rhoades (1998) highlighted a glaring shortcoming in our considerations of higher education by arguing, "One can read most of the higher education literature and not discover that faculty unions exist. One can read many of the most widely read books on higher education and not learn that faculty unions exist. One can get a master's or doctoral degree in many Higher Education programs, and gain no knowledge of faculty unions" (p. 10). Rhoades was writing during a particularly barren period between the initial scholarly interest in unions during the blossoming of collective bargaining in higher education in the 1970s and the renewed attention in the second decade of the 21st century. Yet despite that renewed interest, which is linked to concerns over corporatization and the treatment of the majority of instructional workers who lack the protections of tenure, the larger point remains. As Rhoades and Torres-Olave (2015) recently reiterated when discussing the people who should be among the most knowledgeable, those who study higher education, "Some might even ask, 'Are there any unionized faculty?'" (p. 409). The answer is a resounding yes. The most recent edition of the National Center for the Study of Collective Bargaining in Higher Education and the Profession's (NCSCBHEP) *Directory of U.S. Faculty Contracts and Bargaining Agents in Institutions of Higher Education* (Berry & Savarese, 2012) listed 368,473 faculty members and 64,424 graduate students covered by bargained contracts. The vast majority of the faculty covered were at public institutions (93.6%), more than half whose institution type was known were at 2-year colleges (43.4% at 2-year; 32.7% at 4-year; 17.4% in units that cover both 2- and 4-year institutions) and just over half worked off the tenure track (52%). In all, 27% of college faculty were covered by contracts, in addition to the thousands more who were members of nonbargaining labor unions. Moreover, recent evidence from the NCSCBHEP points to "significant growth" in efforts and bargaining over the past 4 years, with 30 new certified bargaining units in the first 9 months of 2016 alone (Herbert, 2016). These are substantial numbers, and the unionization of faculty and graduate students is a fundamental consideration for stakeholders in U.S. higher education.

That faculty unionization is significant in the modern era should not be surprising—the first faculty union local was founded at Howard University in November 1918 and faculty at dozens of institutions affiliated with the American Federation of Teachers (AFT) in ensuing decades (Cain, 2012b; Lester, 1968). In the late 1940s, the first contracts were negotiated by faculty at Howard and Fisk Universities who were affiliated with the United Public Workers of America (UPWA), although they were not renewed amid concerns over communism in the union (Cain, 2012b). Just over a decade later, faculty unionization fundamentally changed with the passage of enabling legislation in a number of states and legally sanctioned bargaining beginning at institutions such as Milwaukee Technical Institute in 1963, the United States Merchant Marine Academy in 1966, and Bryant College of Business Administration in 1967 (Johnstone, 1981). The dramatic 1966–1967 strike at St. John's University helped spur further interest in unionization (Kugler, 1997), as did successful K–12 bargaining efforts and the broader spirit of activism of the era. Both the National Education Association (NEA) and the American Association of University Professors (AAUP) reevaluated their historic stances against unionization and, by the early 1970s, were actively engaged in organizing college and university faculty for the purpose of collectively bargaining. Bargaining exploded and loomed as a defining feature of higher education in the 1970s (Carnegie Commission on Higher Education, 1973). In 1966, 5,200 instructional workers at 23 institutions operated under bargained contracts, 200 of whom were at the single 4-year institution with a contract. In 1970, 47,300 at 37 colleges did, 23,400 of whom were at the 40 organized 4-year colleges. In 1974, those numbers were 92,300 at 331 institutions, including 60,600 at 132 4-year colleges (Garbarino, 1975). The conditions of faculty work were changing, as they were for other professional workers. Moreover, traditional notions of unions of manual and industrial workers at private corporations are outdated; government workers now make up roughly half of the unionized workforce and education is among the most unionized occupations in the nation (Sproul, Bucklew, & Houghton, 2014; U.S. Bureau of Labor Statistics, 2016).

From the beginning, this move toward unionization in higher education was controversial as early efforts to form nonbargaining locals largely failed to overcome tensions involving appropriateness, status, and professionalization. Whereas some joined a union in hopes of both improving their own lot and fostering larger social equality, others believed joining would reduce their standing and align them with workers rather than the elite professionals whom they viewed as peers. Some viewed unionization as a way to counter the prevailing capitalist ethos and undertake engaged scholarship, whereas others saw it as precluding disinterested research and limiting academic freedom. With the rise of collective bargaining, many of these and other concerns were exacerbated. In light of the recent battles over public sector bargaining in Wisconsin and elsewhere, it is clear that it remains highly contested (Saltzman, 2012).

Stakeholders and observers have articulated positions on either side of the debate over faculty unionization, frequently based on philosophical stances and working assumptions more than substantial data. Advocates argue that unionizing protects academic freedom; provides needed tenure and grievance procedures; offers protection during retrenchment; fosters gender, race, and disciplinary pay equity; provides leverage on compensation and work–life issues; guarantees a faculty voice in governance; serves as a counter to administrative might during periods of corporatization; provides faculty with needed lobbying services; and offers avenues to work for broader change. Opponents counter that it is antithetical to professionalization, mitigates expert judgment, hamstrings institutions, promotes mediocrity over excellence, damages shared governance, precludes academic freedom, diminishes collegiality, centralizes authority, and dismantles faculty status. In *Unionization in the Academy*, DeCew (2003) identified four broad areas of disagreement regarding faculty bargaining:

1. *arguments concerning collegiality on campus and the extent it is enhanced by unions versus arguments claiming that unionization merely incites and increases adversity;*
2. *arguments citing the practical effectiveness of unionization versus those that find unions ineffective, harmful, and a liability on campus;*
3. *arguments about the nature of university and union organizations and whether unions are needed because of a new corporate*

structure at institutions of higher education versus arguments that unions only cause colleges and universities to become more businesslike; and

4. arguments for and against faculty unions based on fundamental academic values. (p. 31)

Embedded within these are questions about whether the challenges of organizing and the costs of unionization—monetary and otherwise—are worth the benefits offered. So, too, are concerns about professional status and identity.

The unionization of graduate students has been even more contentious. Much of the debate—and legal wrangling—involves whether graduate student assistants are primarily students or employees, and whether their teaching assignments, research assistantships, and administrative positions are training or work. Although many maintain that graduate assistantships serve as a form of apprenticeship, Hutchens and Hutchens (2003–2004) called on opponents of graduate unionization to offer "an intellectually credible argument" to "address charges that universities have largely shifted much of the undergraduate teaching load to graduate students in an effort to save money, rather than as the result of careful academic decision-making" (p. 127). Another concern involves how collective bargaining might affect student–faculty relationships, with some arguing that it has the potential to erode them and others contending that it can improve them by removing contentious workplace issues from direct faculty oversight. Opponents suggest that the formalized structures of bargaining, including the grievance procedures that can be adopted, might infringe on faculty judgments in academic and performance issues. Proponents counter that high standards and expert judgment can be retained while simultaneously protecting rights and reducing bias. Additionally, as with faculty unionization, disagreements remain about whether graduate student unions are driving the corporatization of the academy or serving as an explicit response to it (Lee et al., 2004; Rhoades & Rhoads, 2003). In its recent ruling, the NLRB pointed to the work of Rogers, Eaton, and Voos (2013) to note that unionization can actually improve student–faculty relations, but the reaction to its ruling demonstrates that serious disagreement remains. Whereas graduate student petitioners and educational unions lauded the decision as protecting academic freedom and promoting democratic functioning, university administrators expressed concern over changing relationships. The reactions of outside commenters were even more extreme (e.g., Flaherty, 2016a).

About This Monograph

Rhoades's (1998) important point about the lack of awareness of faculty unions should not obscure the fact that scholars—including Rhoades and those he has influenced—have been investigating the reasons for and effects of them for nearly a half century. They have sought to understand how faculty view unionization, correlates with voting behaviors, and reasons for choosing to form and to decertify a union. They have examined contracts and found changes in bargaining over time and have tried to ascertain the effects of unionization on numerous variables including salaries and compensation, campus climate, governance, tenure and grievance procedures, satisfaction, and institutional effectiveness. Although far fewer in number, some scholars have also looked closely at the unionization of graduate students and of non-tenure-line faculty. This monograph examines this research literature on faculty and graduate student unionization in the United States, providing a synthesis of the best evidence of its effects. In so doing, it offers an alternative to arguments over collective bargaining based on bias, supposition, and anecdote.

The second chapter provides on overview of the background and context of faculty and graduate student unionization, highlighting the long history of organizing, the major shift with the rise of collective bargaining, and the uneven distribution of unions across the country and across institution types. The third chapter examines the research on faculty attitudes about unions, both broad views and specific voting behaviors in elections and decertification efforts. The fourth chapter considers studies attempting to understand correlates and effects of tenure-line faculty unionization in areas including compensation, governance, satisfaction, and organizational effectiveness. The fifth and sixth chapters look at the more limited literature on these issues for non-tenure-line faculty and graduate students, respectively. A concluding chapter summarizes what is known about the unionization of instructional workers in U.S. higher education and argues that much more research on campus unions is warranted.

Excepting this introduction and the conclusion, each chapter is organized in consideration of the themes of the literature and chronology of publication, the latter in recognition that the potential issues around and effects of unionization are context and time specific. The literature is drawn almost exclusively from peer-reviewed journals and scholarly books in the fields of higher education and industrial and labor relations; only a few select conference and working papers are included. Several important sources on understanding unionization in higher education fall largely outside of this monograph, perhaps most significantly the dossiers that document the experiences and challenges of organizing and bargaining, and the other firsthand accounts that offer additional ways to understand the local issues and experiences. Additionally, works that focus on legal and legislative aspects or on the processes and strategies of bargaining are largely beyond its scope. So, too, are the many polemical pieces arguing the pros and cons of bargaining or rallying forces in support or opposition to it. Each of these is useful, but the main focus here is on the research literature that attempts to ascertain the effects of bargaining with supporting considerations on how bargaining is viewed by faculty.

In attempting to arrange and convey the literature, I do not advocate for or against faculty or graduate student unionization, although I do agree with the Carnegie Commission on Higher Education's (1973) argument that faculty should have the legally protected right to organize at both public and private institutions. I would add that graduate students should, as well. Public sector unionization is controlled by state law, with some states requiring institutions to bargain when the faculty chooses to, others allowing it but not requiring it, and others explicitly prohibiting it. The details and scope are circumscribed in the state laws and differ accordingly. As is discussed in the next chapter, private faculty unionization is even more limited. Since the Supreme Court's ruling that faculty are managerial employees in *NLRB v.*

Yeshiva University (1980), the ability of tenure-line faculty to organize has been severely limited; most existing unions lost the ability to negotiate and few new ones were later certified. The right to unionize, though, does not always mean that bargaining will be in a particular faculty's best interest. As the literature presented in ensuing chapters shows, the evidence on the effects of unionization is somewhat mixed, especially for tenure-line faculty at 4-year colleges and universities. Much of it is suggestive more than definitive, and many studies lack important elements that could offer clearer understandings, especially as the issues that contribute to unionization—low wages, insecurity, poor relations, etc.—can become conflated with outcomes. Just as important, faculty unionization is simultaneously a local and national phenomenon (Arnold, 2000). Evidence suggesting national outcomes is not necessarily predictive of local ones as each case is particular and affected by local circumstances, personalities, legal and political contexts, and relationships (Julius & DiGiovanni, 2013).

Finally, the way we define terms and identify categories matters, and it can be difficult to find the most appropriate names for different groups of instructional workers, especially those in the majority who work off the tenure track. This is a diverse group that includes full-time lecturers and instructors, part-time workers piecing together multiple positions in an effort to earn a living, external experts brought in to teach applied courses, postdoctoral research and teaching scholars, and many others. A portion of this group is often termed adjunct or contingent, although each of the terms has been criticized for potentially negative connotations and neither captures the breadth of positions that those without a clear route to or the security of tenure possess. As did Kezar and Sam (2010), I recognize that classifying a group in opposition to a more privileged supposed norm—in this case, those eligible for tenure—is inherently problematic. Still, there remains value in having overarching and inclusive terms, so I use tenure-line faculty and non-tenure-line faculty to identify two groups working under fundamentally different conditions. When referring to both groups together, or referencing studies that do not specify, I use faculty without a modifier. Terms such as adjunct and part-time faculty are used only in reference to studies that identify the populations under consideration as such. When I use the term instructional workers, I do so to include tenure-line faculty, non-tenure-line faculty, and graduate students working in teaching roles or otherwise included in bargaining units; non-tenure-line instructors includes non-tenure-line faculty and graduate students. Additionally, throughout this monograph, when used without a modifier, "colleges" refers to both 2- and 4-year institutions.

History and Context

D ESPITE BEING A widespread phenomenon, the unionization of in- structional workers in the United States is often left out of modern considerations of higher education and the professoriate; the longer history of unionization is even more so. Much of the literature that considers it at all conflates the beginning of legally protected bargaining with unionization itself even though unions affected local and national higher education policy for decades prior to the first contracts being signed. Collective bargaining did, though, change the nature and power of unions in higher education, provid- ing new routes to influence campus working conditions and policies. Today, an array of national unions represents faculty and graduate students in for- mal bargaining arrangements, and many more instructional workers bargain without national affiliates. While unionization is extensive, it is not evenly distributed geographically, across institutional types, or across positions. Community colleges, for example, are more heavily unionized than 4-year institutions, public college faculty are more heavily unionized than private college faculty, and graduate students are more likely to be unionized at re- search extensive universities than at those with smaller research footprints.

As background to the larger discussion of the effects of unionization, this chapter traces the trajectory from 29 faculty members in the non- bargaining Howard University Teachers Union to the more than 430,000 instructors currently covered by collectively bargained contracts. It then turns to the current state of bargaining in higher education, identifying key organizational actors, highlighting the regional and institutional variations in bargaining, and pointing to defining features of faculty and graduate student unionization in the second decade of the 21st century.

Historical Backdrop

College faculty unionization began in November 1918 with the founding of a small AFT local at Howard University. It spread to more than 50 college campuses in the politically and economically charged late 1930s before suffering substantial setbacks amid anticommunist purges and defections caused by World War II. After years of struggle, it emerged in the 1960s in a new and stronger form. Emboldened by teacher organizing more broadly, favorable state and federal legislation, and the activism of the decade, faculty turned to collective bargaining as a route to address perceived inequities in a massifying system of higher education. By the early 1970s, when the AAUP and the NEA officially abandoned their long-standing opposition to collective bargaining, it was seen as the key campus trend that would dominate the decade in the manner that student protest had the previous years (Ladd & Lipset, 1973). At the end of the decade, though, the momentum slowed and, in 1980, the Supreme Court of the United States severely hampered the ability of tenure-line faculty at private institutions to bargain. In the 21st century the unionization of college faculty is surging again. Importantly, it is so especially among non-tenure-line and graduate student instructors.

The First Campus Unions

In the early 20th century, a small number of faculty called for unionization as a reasonable response to the increased corporatization of higher education. These appeals took on new importance as the country approached entry into World War I. With the AAUP's founding as a professional association, faculty began to take active steps toward protecting their rights and status, although that organization was opposed to unionization. In 1916, though, the AFT was founded through the affiliation of a handful of existing teachers' unions and, in 1918, as part of a larger effort to expand membership, the union constitution was amended to allow for college faculty unions (Murphy, 1990; Turner, 1919). Several months later, in the days after World War I ended, some of the faculty at Howard University took inspiration from the success-ful war effort and sought to end autocracy in their own institution. The new local was infused with a spirit of democracy and informed by the significant financial struggles that Howard experienced. Its main activity was lobbying Congress for increased appropriations to the federally supported institution, an effort that the university at first approved of but then countered because of fears that it would do more harm than good. Indeed, amid the red scare that followed World War I, the institution found itself under constant surveillance and was fearful of any activity that appeared to be too radical. This fear, along with the local's inability to apply pressure for change in the larger institution, caused it to fold in 1920 without being able to overcome the "degradation of the faculty" that its first secretary, Walter Dyson, later identified (Cain, 2012b; Dyson, 1941, p. 96).

The issues at Howard were shared by faculty at other institutions, includ-ing at the University of Illinois, where faculty founded the second college local in early 1919 in hopes of improving both their remuneration and the institu-tion's governance. They, too, were met with resistance. The combination of improved state largess, which helped alleviate the salary concerns, resistance from faculty who believed that unionization was antithetical to professional status, and an administration that sought to remove union leaders, caused the second AFT local to meet the same fate as the first. Indeed, of the 20 locals founded on colleges and normal schools, or that explicitly included college faculty, all but one closed before 1923. That one, at Milwaukee State Normal School, soon to become Milwaukee State Teachers College, was hampered by the dismissal of its president, Lucius T. Gould, but was able to survive in a skeletal form until the reemergence of faculty unions at the end of the decade. This demise of the first wave of campus locals was both tied to the larger strug-gles of the AFT in the period and specific to higher education. Individual and institutional concerns over leftist politics amid the First Red Scare, attacks on the AFT by the NEA, and the American Federation of Labor's (AFL) with-drawal of support for organizing educators all took tolls on the larger union, most significantly on the faculty locals (Cain, 2010).

Only late in the 1920s, then more so in the 1930s, did the union rebound, growing to 7,500 members in 1934 and 32,000 in 1940. This reemergence of teachers unions was influenced by larger Depression-related changes in U.S. society and labor, as well as the enflamed international scene. In higher education, it began with founding of a small local at Yale University in 1928 designed to provide support for the union movement and AFT, rather than to address any institutional issues. The local would, however, later become embroiled in one of the most significant academic freedom cases of the decade—that involving the 1937 dismissal of local founder and AFT president Jerome Davis. More than 50 additional locals for or including college faculty opened in the 1930s. Some had little focus at their start and struggled to find activities that would generate interest and membership; many were politically active and interested in broad social and economic issues. They fought for academic freedom, tenure, and the rights of educators across sectors and ranks. Many of the locals were small, and none had the ability to collectively bargain, yet some, such as that at the University of Wisconsin, could play significant campus and community roles. Just as important, the organizing efforts attracted attention, including from the AAUP, which retained its professional, antiunion stance. The AFT's increasing success in attracting junior faculty to its more activist approach helped set the context and apply the pressure that led the AAUP and the Association of American Colleges (AAC) to convene the negotiations that would ultimately lead to their joint *1940 Statement on Academic Freedom and Tenure*, perhaps the most important statement on faculty issues in the history of American higher education (Cain, 2012a).

Murphy (1990) argued that the 1930s was a contentious period for the AFT but also one that resulted in a transition from a "gadfly" union emphasizing social issues to one more focused on working conditions and teachers' lives. The experiences of faculty in the AFT underscored that it was a difficult and complicated transition that raised fundamental questions about the purposes and processes of unionization. The period also pointed to issues of stratification and elitism among educators. Many college professors rejected unionism as antithetical to professionalism, yet simultaneously struggled to reach the standards of living that both they and society expected them to maintain. Amid institutional change, college faculty were further differentiating themselves from school teachers. Some longed to ameliorate these divisions but others sought to further the distinctions. Additionally, the union itself was at times conflicted over the role and place of the campus unions. Where leading scholars such as Columbia University's John Dewey and George S. Counts could add prestige to the organization, the graduate students and instructors who made up the majority of many of the locals were problematic to some, especially as they were often at the left edge of a union increasing torn over potential Communist Party domination of some of its locals (Cain, 2012c).

Struggles over communism decimated college faculty unionization in the late-1930s and continued to plague it for years. In 1939, the nonaggression pact between Nazi Germany and the Soviet Union split the American left, including many campus locals, which saw significant drops in membership as the Popular Front against fascism broke. In 1941, the AFT expelled three locals, including the New York College Teachers Union (AFT Local 537), for alleged communist domination. It was a decision that not only removed the single largest college local but also alienated many of those that remained (Cain, 2012c). World War II then further gutted the AFT campus locals as many devoted their energies to war efforts. From 1940 to 1945, officially recognized college locals lost 80% of their membership and many shut down permanently or limped along with little influence (Lester, 1968). Two of the most active AFT college locals in the immediate postwar period soon closed, as well. The local at the University of Washington was expelled for its communist political activity in 1948, whereas Local 223 at the University of Wisconsin shut down in the early 1950s after achieving many of its goals (Lester, 1968; Sanders, 1979). As Lester (1968) argued in her history of faculty in the union, "the college locals had gone from a position of considerable influence and stature in the late 1930s to one of relative unimportance in the AFT" (p. 141).

Despite these declines, interest in higher education unions remained and some of it foreshadowed the coming changes. In 1944, the AFT local at Howard University closed but was replaced by the Howard Branch of the United Federal Workers of America (UFWA), affiliated with the Congress of Industrial Organizations (CIO). The following October, by which time more than two thirds of the university's employees and over half of the faculty had joined, the board of trustees recognized its right to unionize and soon bargained with the nonteaching shop of the union. In February 1947, in an election overseen by the NLRB, the faculty at Howard University voted by a margin of 130 to 1 to be represented by the United Public Workers of America (UPW-CIO), the successor to the UFWA. Welcomed by the university administration, the union negotiated its first contract—and the first known contract of its type in U.S. higher education—later that spring. Faculty at Fisk University soon followed suit but amid the CIO's own push to eliminate communist unions and the increasing legislative attacks on public workers, the CIO expelled the UPW in 1950 and the first contracts were allowed to expire (Cain, 2012b). Although the AFT struggled, it was likewise looking to bargaining. In 1947, faculty at Tri-State College in Angola, Indiana, formed an AFT local and reached out to the national for assistance in their bargaining efforts. Details are vague but the institution contacted the AFT to verify that it was an official union local as it prepared to negotiate and soon instituted a new salary schedule with increases for the faculty. Demonstrating the tenuous nature of unions without legal protections, when the local tried to bargain for a new salary schedule in 1951, the institution's new president denied that it had representation rights (AFT Inventories, 1947–1951; Lester, 1968).

Rise of Bargaining

The events at Howard, Fisk, and Tri-State pointed to the new future for unions in U.S. higher education but the change was not immediate. After the demise of the UPW-CIO, the AFT was the only union involved in organizing teachers and faculty but was still in its "transitional" period as it shifted focus to workplace issues (Lester, 1968, p. 143). Both the AFT and NEA—as yet a professional society whose leadership opposed unionization—experienced increased militancy in some cities in the late 1940s but the pressures of anticommunism that affected campus locals took a broader toll. Both struggled with civil rights and desegregation as well, if in different ways (Murphy, 1990). Still, in the mid-1950s, the AFT formally committed to, in the words of vice president Herrick S. Roth, replacing "collective begging with collective bargaining in order to obtain adequate salaries and suitable working conditions" (Megel, 1956, p. 11). The shift was "a slow, often discouraging, and sometimes extraordinarily frustrating battle of wits between young, dedicated, idealistic organizers and a stubbornly ensconced bureaucracy that was bent on ignoring them" but slow advances were made (Murphy, 1990, p. 211). Then, in 1959, Wisconsin passed the first law allowing public employees to collectively bargain. President John F. Kennedy's executive order 10,988 in 1962 gave federal employees that right and, by 1966, six more states had followed suit (Murphy, 1990). By 1970, 20 states had passed enabling legislation (Lyons, 2008).

These legal protections were brought on by—and in turn helped foster—an era in which the very terms and scope of unionization changed. It was, as Wisconsin Federation of Teachers' President, William Herziger (1967) wrote to a revived AFT local at the University of Wisconsin, an "era of collective bargaining" that brought not only new opportunities but also "new and complex problems." One catalyst for the mass unionization of educational workers was the successful effort of New York K–12 teachers to organize and negotiate a contract. Beginning with the first strike in New York schools in 1960, AFT Local 2 was able to overcome institutional and political resistance to become the bargaining agent for New York teachers. Its settlement of a much larger strike in 1962 fundamentally affected public sector unionization, provided teachers with the inspiration to challenge antistrike legislation in other states, and fostered a great expansion of public and white-collar unionization nationally (Murphy, 1990). For college faculty, it was an indication of a burgeoning labor movement that had the potential to help them counter the difficulties that they faced in growing and increasingly bureaucratic institutions of higher education. Faculty at Milwaukee Technical Institute operated under a bargained contract as part of a larger district including K–12 schools beginning in 1963 (Garbarino, 1975) but perhaps the key event at the college level was a strike by the United Federation of College Teachers (AFT Local 1460) at St. John's University in 1966. The strike was instigated after the dismissal of 31 faculty members for their efforts to garner salary increases and lasted for more than 6 months before the union refocused its efforts on finding the aggrieved faculty positions elsewhere. The strike became a rallying point for organizing on college campuses and a specific spur for more aggressive action in New York and elsewhere. Indeed, in ensuing months, locals at other New York colleges and universities were chartered with specific reference to the St. John's militancy (Kugler, 1997; Lester, 1968; Scimecca & Damiano, 1967).

Shortly after the St. John's strike, faculty at other colleges sought similar routes to protecting their interests. In September 1966, less than a year after gaining the right to collectively bargain, faculty at Henry Ford Community College struck for 6 days and received a new contract with provisions for substantial raises, sabbaticals, and grievance procedures. In Chicago's City Colleges, the Cook County College Teachers Union (AFT Local 1600) struck at the end of 1966 and the beginning of 1967, before securing a new contract that provided for salary increases, seniority rights, limitations to contact hours, and improvements in shared governance. At about the same time, faculty at Lake Michigan Community College earned a new contract after a 6-week strike. The United States Merchant Marine Academy became the first 4-year college to be represented by the AFT in collective negotiations, eventually garnering a contract in early 1968; Bryant College of Business started later but earned its contract in the summer of 1967. With these successes and a larger context that supported white-collar unionization more than at any previous time in U.S. history, the AFT launched a major college organizing drive, advocating for academic freedom, shared governance, and increased salaries. At the end of 1969, faculty at 21 two-year colleges, 2 four-year colleges, and the 19 colleges of the City University of New York were represented by the AFT in collective bargaining. Graduate students at a handful of institutions likewise organized under the AFT, with the local at the University of Wisconsin being the most successful (Hutcheson, 2000; Johnstone, 1981; Lester, 1968).

Amid this changing landscape, the NEA and AAUP, professional organizations that had long forsaken unionization as antithetical to the professional ideal, reconsidered and shifted their models and approaches. The NEA underwent its transition beginning in the early 1960s, evolving from an administrator-led association emphasizing "professional negotiations" to an association fully supportive of collective bargaining, although one that has remained steadfastly outside of the AFL-CIO umbrella. It quickly came to represent faculty at more institutions than either the AFT or the AAUP although its entrance was at first hesitant. Still, in 1971, the organization partnered with the American Federation of State County and Municipal Employees (AFSCME) to form the Coalition of American Public Employees and thereby more closely align itself with labor. The AAUP's entrance into bargaining came in response to the AFT's militancy and its members' own evolving views but also in response to faculty at Belleville College in Illinois choosing the AAUP as a bargaining agent without approval from the national AAUP in 1967. Over the ensuing years, the association haltingly became involved in collective bargaining, eventually endorsing it by a wide margin at its 1972 annual meeting. The following year, the association released its "Statement on Collective Bargaining" and sought a more active role (Benjamin & Mauer, 2006; Hutcheson, 2000).

These organizational efforts bore fruit as faculty unionized at substantial rates in the 1970s, including at private colleges after the NLRB provided them with collective bargaining rights in 1970. The causes for this rise included enabling legislation, the handful of successful negotiations and strikes in the late 1960s, and the broader spirit of protest that had captured U.S. higher education and, to a certain extent, society. The causes extended to the changing conditions of faculty work and of higher education. Certainly, financial concerns were at the heart of this growth of unionization as faculty salaries experienced consecutive years of real declines in the late 1960s and early 1970s. This concern was exacerbated as K–12 teachers saw their salaries rise and faculty began comparing their remuneration and experiences with those of organized teachers. The expansion of higher education, including the growth of multi-campus systems and a perceived rise in stratification and bureaucracy within institutions and systems, likewise contributed, especially as the growth took place mostly at community and former teachers colleges, which had fewer resources and were less likely to have a culture of shared governance. Perceptions of increased adversity on college campuses were important as well (Ladd & Lipset, 1973). Together, these local and national situations led to approximately 25–30% of all faculty being covered by bargained contracts by 1979, a number that included faculty at roughly 20% of all institutions of higher education in the country (Garbarino & Lawler, 1979).

Of course, the instructional workforce was differentiated and the rules for and experiences of bargaining were not the same for those in different positions and places. Bargaining continued to be more likely at 2-year institutions than at 4-year institutions, and among full-time faculty than among part-time faculty. At the beginning of collective bargaining, the diverse mix of instructional workers could be included in many of the same bargaining units, which was at times controversial. In 1972, the NLRB ruled that graduate assistants at private institutions did not have faculty standing and did not share a community of interest with faculty, thereby excluding them from faculty units. Many of the states that allowed bargaining followed suit. Teaching assistants at CUNY and Rutgers, however, remained part of larger units. The following year, the NLRB overturned an earlier precedent and ruled that full-time and part-time faculty did not share a community of interest and were therefore relegated to separate units in private higher education. Labor relations boards in states allowing bargaining ruled variously on the unit makeup, but when excluded from larger units, part-time faculty found it difficult to organize on their own (Saltzman, 2000).

The chartering of new locals slowed dramatically in the last 2 years of the 1970s, at least in part because there was little new state-level enabling legislation. Moreover, two of the most significant attempts to unionize in the latter part of the decade—at the University of Minnesota, Twin Cities and at Michigan State University—failed (Garbarino & Lawler, 1979). Even the small gains in graduate student unionization were dealt a setback when the University of Wisconsin refused to renew contracts with its Teaching Assistants Association after almost a decade of a bargaining relationship. In 1980, efforts to expand faculty unionization met an even more significant challenge when the Supreme Court of the United States issued its ruling in *NLRB v. Yeshiva University*. The court ruled that faculty at Yeshiva held sufficient managerial power so as to be classified as management, rather than employees, and were therefore precluded from unionizing. The ruling fundamentally changed the nature and experience of faculty unionization in U.S. private colleges and universities, led to the decertification of many locals, and largely reverted private college locals to the advocacy and activism model that had existed prior to bargaining (DeCew, 2003; Douglas, 1990; Hurd & Foerster, 1996; Metchick & Singh, 2004; *NLRB v. Yeshiva*, 1980; Thomas & McGehee, 1994).

The National Center on Collective Bargaining in Higher Education's then-annual directories of contracts and agents highlight the slow growth in bargaining in higher education in the 1980s and 1990s, as well as shifts in who was being organized. Douglas (1984), for example, called the organizing of new locals "virtually nonexistent," while also reporting five Yeshiva-related union decertifications. Four years later, he wrote, "Modest increases were reported in virtually every category used to record collective bargaining in higher education (CBHE), however, for the first time since the Center began tabulating such data in 1974, no bargaining units consisting of full-time, tenure-track faculty were organized. Of the four new bargaining units in which agents were elected in 1987, three consisted of part-time faculty and one of teaching assistants" (Douglas, 1988, p. v). Overall, the number of bargaining agents for full- and part-time faculty grew from 427 in 1980 to 460 in 1990 and the number of contracts from 359 to 440. Much of this growth was at 2-year institutions, where the number of agents and contracts grew from 276 to 311 and 236 to 317, respectively. At 4-year institutions, the number of agents dropped from 151 to 143, whereas the number of contracts rose from 123 to 129 (Hurd & Foerster, 1996).

The unionization of faculty continued to slowly expand but by the end of the 20th century, much of the most intense interest and activity involved graduate students (DeCew, 2003). The 1990s and early 2000s saw graduate students at numerous public and private universities organize in attempts to bargain for better working conditions and wages. At institutions such as the Universities of California and Illinois, they struck and, eventually, won recognition from their institutions. Significant and lengthy organizing efforts also took place at Yale University and New York University (NYU), both playing out in the press and highlighting competing conceptions of the purposes of graduate assistantships, the roles of students as laborers, and the contentious nature of graduate student organizing. These efforts were complicated by varying rulings on students' eligibility to bargain (DeCew, 2003; Krause, Nolan, Palm, & Ross, 2008; Nelson, 1997; Saltzman, 2000). Between 1969 and 1994, 12 graduate student units were organized, which by 2005, contained 21,333 graduate students, or 34.7% of those covered by bargained contracts. From 1995 to 1999, five more units were established containing 17,700 members (31.0%). Between 2000 and 2005, nine additional units with 18,012 members (31.6%) were organized (Moriarty & Savarese, 2006).

At the turn of the century and in the years since, significant attention has been paid to the large and growing percentage of faculty working off the tenure track, and substantial efforts have been made to unionize lecturers, postdoctoral scholars, and adjunct laborers, including on citywide bases. From 1998 to 2012, the number of unionized part-time and adjunct faculty members almost doubled from 75,882 to 147,021 (Julius & DiGiovanni, 2013). In these efforts for non-tenure-line faculty and graduate students, the existing bargaining agents have been joined by additional unions, most prominently the United Automobile, Aerospace, and Agricultural Implement Workers of America (UAW) and the Service Employees International Union, both of which organize laborers across numerous industries, including nonacademic workers in higher education.

Current Landscape

In the most recent directory Berry and Savarese (2012) list 368,473 part-time and full-time faculty represented for collective bargaining by 639 agents at 1,174 campuses of 519 institutions and systems. An additional 64,424 graduate students at 30 institutions or systems were represented. These are significant numbers that are further discussed later, but they must be used with caution, because of age, difficulties in gathering data, and data that are impossible to disaggregate—for example, an unknown, though presumably small, number of individuals who would not normally be considered faculty are included in some of the bargaining units. Moreover, because of nonresponses, the authors were required to estimate the membership in almost one third of the bargaining units, relying on data from 1998 and 2006, as well as other sources. The changing legal landscape that has made public sector bargaining more difficult in some states has potentially affected the numbers in substantial ways, as has the push forward of non-tenure-line faculty unionization in recent years. Still, the directory offers the best evidence of the scope and distribution of bargaining in higher education.

According to Berry and Savarese (2012), 27% of the faculty in the United States were represented by a bargaining agent, though there are significant differences in the rates of unionizing by institution type, location, and position.

Public 2-year colleges were the most heavily unionized, with 160,062 faculty (42% of their total faculty) represented by bargaining agents. Public 4-year colleges included 120,672 represented faculty (25% of their total faculty), whereas an additional 64,028 public college faculty were in units that include both 2- and 4-year colleges. At private colleges, 20,135 faculty were unionized, almost all at 4-year not-for-profit institutions, where unionized faculty comprised 7% of the total faculty. Among 4-year institutions, unionization was far more prevalent at comprehensive colleges and universities than at either baccalaureate institutions or research universities.

Of the 315,357 represented faculty whose status was known, 168,336 were full time and 147,021 were part time. Those numbers were 26% and 21% of the National Center for Education Statistics's (NCES) numbers of full- and part-time faculty, respectively. Fifty-three percent of represented faculty (167,074) whose status was known were non-tenure line; 47% (148,283) were tenure line (Berry & Savarese, 2012). With state law controlling public sector unionizing, there are significant differences in bargaining by state. California (25%) and New York (23%) were home to almost half of all faculty represented by bargaining agents and just nine states accounted for 80% of represented faculty. No faculty were represented by bargaining agents in 19 states, including the entire southeast except Florida and much of the southwest (Berry & Savarese, 2012).

According to Berry and Savarese (2012), graduate students were represented on 92 campuses of 30 universities or systems. All of the represented graduate students were at public 4-year universities in one of the 14 states; more than half were in California (31%), Florida (14%), and Illinois (10%). The 64,424 graduate students represent 20% of the total number of graduate student employees in NCES and 25% of those at public universities. Again, these numbers are useful but the overall situation may now be somewhat different. For example, the numbers included graduate students at the University of Wisconsin who no longer bargain because of changes in state law, but not those at New York University, which in 2013 voluntarily entered into bargaining with its graduate students after many years of resisting it. Differences in patterns of faculty and graduate student organizing include that tenure-line faculty unions are rarely found in selective research universities, but many of the 30 graduate student unions represented by a bargaining agent are at such institutions. Graduate students at many more are in the process of organizing and will likely be emboldened by the recent Columbia NLRB ruling. Additionally, the vast majority of faculty were represented by some combination of the AAUP, AFT, and NEA (82%) but just more than half of represented graduate students were in units affiliated with the UAW (43%), Communication Workers of America (CWA; 6%), and United Electrical, Radio and Machine Workers (UE; 4%).

National Organizations

As noted, the majority of faculty bargaining agents are affiliated with one or more of three national organizations: the AAUP, the AFT, or the NEA. They are joined by smaller numbers of instructional workers in the SEIU, UAW, CWA, AFSCME, and the American Federation of Government Employees (AFGE), as well as the roughly 7% who bargain without national affiliations. Graduate students are much more likely to be affiliated with industrial unions than are faculty, especially tenure-line faculty. Although the national organizations have grown somewhat more similar over time and have worked together to varying degrees at both individual institutions and larger national efforts, each has its own character.

Founded in 1915, the modern AAUP retains its long-standing commitments to academic freedom, tenure, and shared governance, both in the context of its bargaining roles and beyond. After a recent restructuring, it is now composed of three related but distinct units: the historic professional association emphasizing academic freedom, tenure, shared governance, and related issues; the American Association of University Professors Collective Bargaining Congress, which serves as the union; and the AAUP Foundation, a nonprofit charitable organization. Approximately three quarters of its approximately 47,000 members are in collective bargaining units (Finkelstein, Conley, & Schuster, 2016; Schmidt, 2014a). Berry and Savarese (2012) identified 31,195 faculty represented by 62 AAUP units on 107 campuses, along with thousands more in units affiliated with both the AAUP and other national organizations, many of which were in the California State University System. The AAUP currently claims more than 80 bargaining affiliates, mostly representing tenure-line faculty at 4-year institutions or systems. In defining its bargaining activity, it emphasizes its long-standing commitment to and sole focus on higher education, the importance of academic freedom and tenure, the autonomy of local affiliates, and a "dedication to organizational democracy" (AAUP, 2005). In recent years, internal shifts and leadership election results have led to more activist stances by the AAUP and further commitment to organizing as a primary—to some critics, overemphasized—function (Schmidt, 2014a, 2014b).

The AFT is the historic teachers union affiliated with the AFL-CIO and its activities helped lead to the modern era of collective bargaining. It currently counts more than 1,600,000 educators as members (http://rishawnbiddle.org/outsidereports/aft_2015_dol_filing.pdf), approximately 200,000 of whom work in a variety of positions across higher education sectors. Its early bargaining efforts emphasized traditional union goals, including compensation and security of positions, both of which maintain prominence in the union's efforts. The union has likewise identified pay equity, academic freedom, increased faculty diversity, reversing the trends of increased reliance on non-tenure-line faculty, providing protections and tenure-line hiring preferences for current non-tenure-line faculty, and holding for-profit institutions accountable as among its higher education goals.

Dating to 1857, the NEA was long a professional association emphasizing K–12 education, despite the presence of higher education leaders in its early decades. It fully embraced bargaining by the early 1970s, billing itself as an independent and professional alternative to the AFL-CIO-affiliated AFT. With roughly three million members, including more than 200,000 in positions in higher education (http://www.nea.org/home/34718.htm), the NEA is by far the largest of the three main bargaining organizations for educators. It identifies key issues as academic freedom, tenure, higher education funding, the reliance on non-tenure-line faculty, the shift toward distance education, and intellectual property. In addition to producing publications such as *Thought & Action* and *the NEA Almanac of Higher Education*, the union sponsors the

National Council for Higher Education, an independent membership organization focused on higher education policy and advocacy.

The other groups organizing higher educational instructional staff do so on a smaller scale, though several have been quite active in recent years. SEIU is a union of almost two million workers in the service and related industries, such as healthcare, childcare, and maintenance work. It has made significant inroads into organizing non-tenure-line faculty through its Adjunct Action campaign and its more recent Faculty Forward campaign, including tenure-line faculty, non-tenure-line faculty, and graduate students. Faculty Forward's broader goals include $15,000 in per course compensation, greater accountability for for-profit institutions, and increased affordability of higher education (Flaherty, 2015). Berry and Savarese (2012) identified 32,000 covered faculty/instructors affiliated with SEIU either exclusively or mutually with other unions, most of whom were in the California State University System. Faculty Forward currently claims 120,000 higher education workers as part of its efforts, though not all are members of the union and some who are have not won bargaining elections. Although non-tenure-line faculty at more than 40 institutions are members, some units, such as those at Notre Dame de Namur, which has recently won bargaining rights, include both tenure-line and non-tenure-line faculty (http://seiufacultyforward.org/why-seiu/).

The UAW, the historic autoworkers union that disaffiliated from the AFL-CIO in 1968, has been involved in higher education for more than 30 years. Many of its efforts involve administrative and clerical workers but since the 1981 affiliation and then 1987 merger of District 65, which organized teaching assistants at the University of California among others, instructional staff members have been in the union as well (Eidlin, 2016; Prial, 1987). The UAW has been an important actor in organizing graduate students, postdoctoral associates, and non-tenure-line faculty, especially on the west coast and in the northeast.

Other unions have smaller footprints among the instructional staffs. The CWA represents 700,000 workers in the United States, Canada, and Puerto Rico across information, communications, technology, law enforcement, and related fields. Among its units is CWA Public, Healthcare and Education Workers, representing 140,000 workers in a range of positions, including some in teaching positions. In higher education, most of its membership is made up of graduate students at the State University of New York, though it also represents faculty on a handful of campuses. In 1995, the Campaign to Organize Graduate Students at the University of Iowa affiliated with UE, a union of 35,000 members, because of its progressive history of democratic unionism and public sector success in the state. The following spring, it won bargaining rights (http://www.ueunion.org/uewho.html; http://cogs.org/about-cogs/history; Scott, 2000). AFSCME, a union of 1.6 million members and retirees almost exclusively in the public sector, represents faculty at Central Connecticut, adult educators at the City Colleges of Chicago, and the faculty of the for-profit Art Institute of Philadelphia (http://www.afscme.org/union/about; Berry & Savarese, 2012).

Conclusion

The unionization of instructional workers in higher education has changed fundamentally in the almost 100 years since faculty formed the first AFT college local. First met with bewilderment and condescension, by the 1930s faculty and graduate student unions affected local campus decisions and larger national policy discussions. The rise of bargaining, briefly in the late 1940s and then much more when legally protected in the 1960s, changed the nature and practice of unionization. Bargaining spread dramatically in the early 1970s but then stagnated, especially at 4-year institutions, amid adverse legal rulings and with a hiatus new state-level enabling legislation. Unionization picked up in the late-1990s and early 2000s, especially among graduate students and non-tenure-line faculty despite an often hostile political environment. Both remain at the heart of ongoing organizing efforts, though recent years have also seen increased interest in organizing at research universities. Of course, unionization remains highly differentiated by institutional type, position, and region. Yet with more than 400,000 instructional workers operating under bargained contracts, it is a key feature of American higher education, if one that is not always recognized or understood.

The Attitudes and Voting Behaviors of Tenure-Line Faculty

FACULTY UNIONIZATION HAS been contested since the earliest nonbargaining locals sought to bridge class divides and unite the "hand worker" with the "head worker," and it has remained so in the modern era of collective bargaining. For more than four decades, scholars have sought to understand faculty attitudes toward bargaining and correlates with actual or intended voting behavior. They have proposed numerous explanations for decisions to unionize that speak to both local and national issues and have highlighted the effects of changing attitudes toward unionization more broadly, concerns over governance and remuneration, and status issues both within the faculty and in relation to other workers. They have examined the relationship between union attitudes and characteristics such as career stage, disciplinary affiliation, satisfaction, age, and, to a lesser extent, race and gender. And they have looked beyond views on unionization to actual voting patterns and, in a few cases, militancy. Much of the portrait offered is what might be expected: faculty who identify as more liberal or are less satisfied with salary or governance, for example, are more likely to support collective bargaining. Moreover, these studies can necessarily tell only part of the story of the growth of unionization. Both local conditions and larger structural factors influence the ability of faculty to unionize, even when they are so inclined. Also, as Kemerer and Baldridge (1975) argued, "It is possible to believe in unions but refuse to join one. Alternatively, one can have a lukewarm attitude toward collective bargaining in general but be very involved in the union movement because of environmental and institutional conditions" (pp. 62–63).

This chapter examines the published research on faculty attitudes toward collective bargaining both generally and with regard to their own real and hypothetical voting behaviors. As do the chapters that follow, it does so largely chronologically from the early 1970s through the second decade of the 20th century. When viewed this way, the patterns in the literature can be seen: early interest in attitudes about unionization in relation to demographic characteristics and political attitudes gave way to studies that more directly focused on economic and noneconomic factors related to union attitudes, including perceptions of senate, administrative, and potential union power. These later studies often used more advanced methods, as might be expected, but did so on smaller scales. Over time, the interest waned and all but disappeared. This review found no studies specifically on attitudes and voting published from 2000–2008 and only a handful in the years since.

Early Considerations of Attitudes and Attributes

Large-scale investigations of faculty attitudes regarding bargaining date at least to a 1969 survey undertaken by the Carnegie Commission on Higher Education and the American Council on Education. The survey of more than 60,000 faculty across institution types and ranks (including lecturer and instructor, as well as ladder ranks) covered a broad array of topics, including views on governance, salaries, and political orientation. The weighted results included that only a minority of faculty members (40.1%) agreed either strongly or with reservations with the statement "Collective bargaining by faculty members has no place in a college or university," with fewer agreeing at 4-year colleges than at universities, and even fewer agreeing at 2-year colleges. Still, just over half (52.5%) agreed that "faculty unions have a divisive effect on academic life," a finding that was consistent across institutional types (Bayer, 1970, p. 18). A partial replication in 1972–1973 yielded more than 42,000 responses and found even further openness to bargaining among faculty: only 34.1% believed that there was no place for bargaining in colleges and universities. Again, 2-year faculty were the least likely to agree, followed by 4-year college faculty (Bayer, 1973).

The 1969 survey results were further analyzed in numerous ways around a range of faculty issues, including collective bargaining (Bayer, 1973). Carr and Van Eyck (1973) used them to highlight that nontenured faculty were more likely to support bargaining than were tenured, and faculty who supported bargaining were more likely to be dissatisfied with elements of academic governance such as the power of senior professors and the effectiveness of the faculty senate. More substantially, as part of their landmark study, Ladd and Lipset (1973) presented additional data from the 1969 survey, including that 47% of respondents agreed either strongly or with reservations that "faculty strikes can be legitimate" (p. 12). Their results show that faculty who were younger, without tenure, had lower salaries, and worked at less elite institutions were more likely to view strikes as legitimate. The more liberal and in support of both student activism and faculty governance the respondents, the more likely they were to support both bargaining and strikes. Surprising to Ladd and Lipset, despite these overall trends, faculty at more elite institutions were the ones most critical of governance, suggesting that it was not the governance issues that were driving the support for bargaining at less elite colleges.

Ladd and Lipset also presented data from a 1972 follow-up phone survey of almost 500 four-year college faculty, including that 43% of faculty agreed that the growth in bargaining was beneficial and should be extended, that 44% disagreed and 13% were conflicted. Again younger and more liberal faculty were more likely to support collective bargaining. They found no evidence that differences in socioeconomic class backgrounds affected support for unions, but Jewish faculty were more likely to support unions than non-Jewish faculty. Disciplinary differences were found in both surveys, with social science faculty being the most likely to both identify as liberal/left and support unions, followed by those in the humanities and natural sciences. Business and applied faculty were the least likely. In their full analysis, Ladd and Lipset pointed to two separate sources for support for faculty bargaining:

Large, apparently growing, segments of the professoriate occupy positions that give them kind of a "class interest" in the development

*of unionism. They are at institutions where faculty have less pro-
fessional independence, are poorly compensated economically, or receive low recognition.... At the same time, views on unionism are
a function of general ideological orientations. (p. 25)*

These views and statuses could often work at cross-purposes, as faculty at
elite institutions with higher professional status were often the most liberal.
To Ladd and Lipset, the local conditions and "objective interests" were often
determinant when these faculty were deciding on whether to join (p. 32).

As part of the Stanford Project on Academic Governance, Frank R.
Kemerer and J. Victor Baldridge undertook large surveys of administrators
and faculty in 1971 and 1973, eventually publishing their results in multiple forms (e.g., Baldridge & Kemerer, 1976; Kemerer & Baldridge, 1975).
The latter survey was focused specifically on bargaining and directed at presidents and union bargaining unit chairs; it was supplemented with campus case
studies. Their findings pointed to the "strong environmental forces" (1975,
p. 4) fostering the rise of unionization, most notably the economic crisis of
the period and an end to the explosive growth of faculty positions of the previous decade. They likewise highlighted the importance of governance considerations to faculty views on bargaining, including that institutions with
new and weak senates were more likely to have faculty who supported bargaining. Their results confirmed and extended some earlier studies, including
that faculty at elite institutions and private institutions were less likely to support unionization. Faculty who perceived high levels of external influence and
who were at new institutions were more likely to support it. Younger, more
junior, and male faculty were again more likely to support unionization but,
in the Stanford study, faculty with more advanced degrees were generally less
likely to support bargaining on their campuses. Those in vocational/technical
disciplines were most likely to support unionization, followed by humanities
and social science faculty. As would be expected, faculty who trusted and had
confidence in their administrations were far less likely to seek collective bargaining than those who did not.

For the remainder of the pre-*Yeshiva* years studies of faculty attitudes focused more narrowly on single institutions or, in a few cases, a handful of

institutions in a single state. These largely offered similar findings regarding both the broader appeal of unions and specific voting behaviors, though sometimes differed on what the most important local issue was. Among the more significant of these was Haehn's (1970) study of attitudes in the California State Colleges undertaken as part of a broader initiative of the system's academic senate. The 835 usable responses from 18 colleges revealed a preference for collective bargaining across the campuses, with 61% responding that they were moderately or strongly in favor of bargaining; another 18% were unsure. In response to a question asking if the election were "held today," 67% indicated that they would vote for bargaining, 25% against, and the rest would not vote (p. 14). As might be expected, faculty favoring bargaining were less likely to indicate that they believed the faculty senate was effective in influencing policy. Haehn also found that higher percentages of faculty in the liberal arts, younger faculty, faculty who identified as liberal, faculty who identified as Democratic, and faculty who indicated that bargaining was consistent with professionalism were more likely to support bargaining. Full professors were the least likely to favor it among the various ranks; assistant and associate professors' views were nearly identical. Across respondents, regardless of whether they supported bargaining, 78% of faculty members believed that a union could be effective in addressing salary issues. Slightly lower percentages indicated that it could be on fringe benefits (76%) and academic working conditions (74%).

Studies of unionization in the 2- and 4-year colleges and universities in Hawaii point both to original faculty attitudes and changes over time after an initial union was unsuccessful and was decertified. At the time of initial voting, being higher ranked, tenured, older, higher credentialed, and at the most elite campus were associated with less support for collective bargaining overall and, to the extent it was supported, a professional negotiation rather than union bargaining approach. Moving through faculty ranks quickly and being satisfied with departmental administration were likewise associated with lower support for bargaining. Younger and lower status faculty were more likely to support both bargaining overall and a more assertive approach. Education, health and social welfare, humanities, and social science faculty were more supportive of bargaining than those in science and engineering (Kelley, 1979;

Seidman, Edge, & Kelley, 1974; Seidman, Kelley & Edge, 1974a, 1974b). Bargaining difficulties and a decertification of the first union further revealed divides among the faculty (Simson, 1975) but also weakened both the opposition to and support for the union. A 1976 survey revealed that many who had voted against bargaining or for a "professional" approach to it were more supportive of union bargaining, whereas many who had supported the more assertive union contestants in the election had moderated their support (Kelley & Edge, 1976).

Pennsylvania was the site of numerous additional studies, including one of few to focus explicitly on community colleges, even though they were the locus of much early bargaining. Based on his survey of more than 600 faculty at 10 community colleges, Moore (1971) found that faculty who believed they were more mobile; believed that they had little power in the institution; and were younger untenured, lower ranked, male, non-Protestant, better credentialed, more dissatisfied, politically liberal; and taught outside the sciences were more likely to support bargaining than their counterparts

More attention was paid to faculty attitudes in the Pennsylvania State College system, which agreed to its first contract in 1972 but then met in impasse in negotiations in 1974. Before the first election, Flango and Brumbaugh (1972) surveyed more than 800 faculty and found that salary was the most pressing issue but that there were no differences in support for bargaining based on local or cosmopolitan orientation. Based on 140 usable questionnaire responses, Muczyk, Hise, and Gannon (1975) found several differences between faculty favoring bargaining and those not, though few of them were significant at the .05 level. Being in education as opposed to other disciplines, being less satisfied with salary, believing that bargaining would not make it difficult to reward deserving faculty, and believing that a union would not create an adversarial relationship were associated with support for representation. Gable and Coolsen (1975) found few differences in faculty support for a job action among union and nonunion member faculty at a single institution—they differed only in whether an impasse on tenure would warrant a job action—though their sample was small and skewed. Predictably, union members viewed the union and its activities more favorable than nonmembers. Flango (1975) found that economic issues were most important in

Pennsylvania and that those who were most concerned about economic issues showed the least interest in the differences between potential bargaining agents. Lozier and Mortimer (1974a; 1976) found that faculty were more influenced by external state-level concerns than local administrative concerns in their voting to unionize, a further indication of the significance of financial considerations. In a related piece, Lozier and Mortimer (1974b) highlighted some differences between the findings of this survey and one undertaken at Temple University. At Temple, internal factors were more influential than external. The finding highlighted that although larger national patterns exist, local situations are quite important, and perhaps determinant.

Lozier and Mortimer (1974a, 1976) linked Pennsylvania public college faculty's support of bargaining to the teachers college histories of the institutions. Kazlow and Giaquinta (1977) looked specifically at the education faculty of a private university, in part trying to understand militancy. They found education faculty to be more in favor of bargaining and of unionism than the national average. Similar to Lozier and Mortimer, they also found that older and tenured faculty were more likely to support unionism. Although these findings counter some of the larger trends in the literature, they can be explained by the shifting nature of these institutions—long-standing faculty in both studies had experienced significant shifts in their institutions' missions and focuses.

Systemic shifts were also implicated in Hagengruber's (1978) consideration of unionization efforts at the University of Wisconsin that traced splits within the faculty to both economic crisis and the merger of the institution with the state university system. The combined factors led to precariousness, pay dissatisfaction, and perceived loss of power among untenured faculty; for many, this led to support for collective bargaining. Yet full professors remained largely satisfied with their pay and believed that on their campus, as opposed to in a centralizing system, they were well treated. Overall, despite strong interest in bargaining, the majority of the faculty remained committed to traditional shared governance, though used it to more assertively advocate for their economic and political interests. To Hagengruber, institutional status and long-standing governance mechanisms were important factors in the rejection of collective bargaining. In a paired article, Carey (1978) described the efforts to achieve collective bargaining at the University of Massachusetts from his role as a union organizer. Both the severe economic situation, which led to stagnant pay and increased teaching loads, and the lack of power of faculty in institutional governance led faculty, librarians, and academic professionals to overcome the belief that unionization was unprofessional and to choose to bargain. As one faculty member noted, "we'll just have to face the fact we are also employees and have to unionize for our own protection" (p. 85).

Though specifics differed across studies, additional single-site surveys pointed to measures of institutional conditions, employment status, union instrumentality, disciplinary affiliation, pay, dissatisfaction, and distrust in the administration to be associated with support for bargaining (e.g., Bernhardt, 1977; Bigoness, 1978; Driscoll, 1978; Feuille & Blandin, 1974, 1976; Lindeman, 1975; Nixon, 1973, 1975). Gress's (1976) study of faculty at three Ohio institutions found highest degree earned, experience, rank, tenure, compensation, and professional activity to be negatively correlated with attitude toward collective bargaining. The only positive correlation was a measure of perceived severity of campus issues.

Beyond these survey studies, two significant case-based examinations of unionization at multiple institutions revealed faculty concerns over governance and centralization as key motivating factors. Begin, Settle, and Alexander (1977) examined organizing and bargaining across public and private universities in New Jersey, noting the combination of external factors, institutional factors, and faculty characteristics that could play a role. The unionization of K–12 schools, bargaining in other colleges and systems, and competition among the unions themselves, for example, could all foster bargaining, as could significant organizational change or faculty/administration conflict. Lee's (1979) comparative case studies of six institutions—two each of public universities, state colleges, and private liberal arts colleges—emphasized faculty governance roles as the motivator of unionization. Faculty at the universities were "preservationists" (p. 569) who sought to retain their power in the face of increasing centralization, while also seeking to remain distinct from the state colleges and their unions. At the other institutions, unionization was viewed as a route toward formal faculty governance roles where they had not existed before.

By the time of *Yeshiva*, basic patterns in the research findings had been established. Younger and untenured faculty were generally more likely to favor bargaining and more likely to favor more aggressive organizations and tactics, but institutional and system factors could alter this pattern. At institutions that had experienced significant change, such as teachers colleges that had become comprehensive colleges or universities, age and rank could be positively associated with support for unionization. Disciplines and fields mattered, with faculty in the humanities, social sciences, education, and vocational fields more likely to support unions. The role of perceived mobility was unclear. As might be expected, faculty who were more dissatisfied and who believed that unions could be effective, were more likely to support bargaining. Finally, although salary issues were key, by the end of the decade it was clear that concerns over faculty power and governance roles were likewise drivers of unionization, especially in light of perceived centralization of administrative authority.

Economic and Noneconomic Factors in the 1980s

By the end of the decade, more studies drew on organizational and social psychology theory to consider faculty attitudes and voting behaviors, and they did so with more explicit consideration of the relative importance of economic and noneconomic factors. In a pair of studies, one that included multiple institutions and one that did not, Neumann (1979, 1980) built on Gress's (1976) work and considered organizational climate as a potential predictor of faculty views. He found that faculty perceptions of power were the strongest determinants of attitudes toward bargaining, although the specific types of power differed by discipline. In the physical sciences, perceived individual power was negatively correlated with view of collective bargaining, whereas perceived central administrative power was positively correlated. In the social sciences, perceived faculty power was negatively correlated with bargaining, and perceived department chair power was positively correlated.

In their study of more than 1,200 faculty in the California State University and Colleges (CSUC) system, Lawler and Walker (1980) found that faculty who expected positive outcomes from bargaining (improved quality of educational programs and increased resources, equity in personnel decisions, personal efficacy, and salary) were more likely to support bargaining whereas those who expected negative outcomes (decreased influence of senate and increased conflict and power of external groups) were less likely to do so. Those who saw the job market in a positive light were less likely to support bargaining, as were those with high levels of personal efficacy. They argued that "unions serve as a kind of insurance function for employees of an organization, protecting them against arbitrary management policies threatening to an employee's status with the organization" (p. 112). Elsewhere, Lawler and Walker (1979) emphasized issues of power in CSUC faculty choice of bargaining unit, finding that perception of greater power in the administration and less power in the senate was aligned with joining a more activist union. A follow-up study with additional data from a 1981 administration found that voting preferences were established early and that union campaign activities had no discernable effect (Walker & Lawler, 1986).

Hammer and Berman (1981) emphasized issues of power, discontent, and distrust in their study of faculty at a private institution. In their analysis, demographic characteristics were not significant predictors but satisfaction with job content and trust in the administration were negatively correlated with voting for the union. Importantly, satisfaction with economic issues was positively correlated with voting behaviors but only 7.7% of those who voted to unionize ranked salary increases as the most important issue behind faculty decision-making power (42.3%), tenure procedures (25.0%), and grievance procedures (17.3%); it was even with academic freedom.

Yet other work continued to show the importance of salary in faculty attitudes and behaviors, including Allen and Keaveny's (1981) study of 220 faculty at the University of Wyoming. They found that multiple measures related to salary (including satisfaction and the size and perceived equity of increases) were significant predictors of attitudes toward unionization. Rank, tenure, and age were not significant when salary was controlled. In a survey of faculty at Central Michigan University, Dayal (1982) found a somewhat mixed picture. When asked to identify the most important of 20 bargaining goals, 10 of which were economic and 10 of which were not, faculty identified academic freedom as the most important goal, followed by salary, inflation adjustments, hiring standards, and reappointment criteria. Yet when asked which set of goals was more important, 62.4% indicated that economic goals were more important than noneconomic goals. A follow-up survey administration in 1985 again found academic freedom to be the most cited goal, followed by salary and class size; 60% identified economic goals as more important (Dayal, 1986, 1992).

Rather than examining real or hypothetical votes to unionize, Bigoness and Tosi (1984) looked at correlates with voting in a union decertification election at a large public university. Based on 112 survey responses, they found union instrumentality, attitudes toward unions, and being female significantly associated with voting to maintain representation, while salary and measures of satisfaction were not. Dworkin and Lee (1985) used a model developed by Farber and Saks (1980) to examine unionization at a large midwestern university, finding that both "wage and nonwage aspects of the job do impact upon faculty vote intentions" (p. 382). Faculty whose pay was low and those dissatisfied with the fairness of administrative policy were more likely to intend to vote for unionization, as were faculty who reported both that they were not dissatisfied with their job security and would find it difficult to find a similar job. Faculty who were dissatisfied with job security and would find it difficult to find a comparable job were similarly inclined. Women were more likely to intend to vote for unionization.

Zalesney (1985) found that noneconomic factors—especially those related to attitudes toward an organization and bargaining generally, social forces, and perceived efficacy of the bargaining—were better predictors of voting behavior than economic factors at a large midwestern public university. However, two of the three economic factors considered were organizational, with only salary satisfaction measured at the individual level. Bornheimer's (1985) consideration of two votes at New York University in the 1970s revealed that faculty characteristics had little predictive ability, though satisfaction with conditions (academic freedom, governance, etc.) did. In comparing cases of unionization at two institutions in close proximity in New Hampshire, Weed (1987) found that at one, faculty unionized for economic and status reasons; at the other governance issues were most important, followed by salary concerns.

Williams and Zirkel (1989) did not include many of these later pieces in their literature review of 75 studies of attitudes, voting, and contract inclusion but their article still highlighted a larger shift that might help explain the inconsistent findings. They argued that the research "suggests that economic factors were the primary reason for faculty unionization" but that over time, issues covered in contracts evolved to include additional personnel and governance issues. According to their review, this was partly as a result of the diminishing returns to unionization in areas of salary and compensation. Combined with local and institutional factors, then, broader changes in faculty conditions and perceptions complicated any effort at a definitive finding on what drives faculty attitudes and behaviors. So, too, did the prevalence of single institution survey studies.

Small-Scale Studies in the 1990s

The 1990s saw continued interest in the faculty attitudes and voting behaviors regarding unionization, with many studies grounding their understandings in Williams and Zirkel's (1989) emphasis on economic factors. Yet, just as with the much of the earlier research, the studies were mostly small scale and the findings included a range of factors related to attitudes and intent. Crisci, Fisher, Blixt, and Brewer (1990), for example, found that nursing faculty in unions were overall more in favor of bargaining than those who are not in unions. Borstoff, Nye, and Field (1994) looked specifically at a state without bargaining rights and found that membership in the nonbargaining affiliate of the National Education Association was associated with the intent to vote for bargaining, if it became an option. So, too, were job and pay dissatisfaction and positive attitude toward unionization, demographic characteristics were not.

Ali and Karim (1992) and Karim and Ali (1993) identified four sets of issues as the most important correlates: compensation, personnel, governance, and, to a lesser extent, academic concerns. They found that although more respondents to a survey at a nonunionized regional university in Indiana believed that compensation issues had influenced the growth of bargaining than did desire for greater input into governance (79.3% to 64.7%), many believed that unions are more successful in providing personnel protections (86%) and grievance procedures (69.5%) than greater compensation (60.5%). More than half did not believe that a desire to improve academic quality had contributed to the rise of bargaining. They found significant differences in responses based on income, rank, tenure, and gender, though were not clear on the direction of those differences. They found none by discipline.

Using a modified version of the previous survey, Karim and Rassuli (1996) considered personnel, compensation, governance, union image, and job context as factors in their study of 244 faculty at a primarily undergraduate institution in the southwest. They found that faculty again largely agreed that compensation concerns (79%) and a desire for greater control (67%) influenced the growth of bargaining. Majorities again agreed that a union would provide channels for grievances (82%) and protect faculty against arbitrary action (70%). Personnel issues, perception of unions, governance, and compensation beliefs, as well as demographic factors, were significantly associated with union voting. In a more complex, though still single institution, study, Rassuli, Karim, and Roy (1999) attempted to ascertain how faculty views on bargaining changed before an election and in its aftermath, considering personnel, compensation, governance, union image, and job context as factors affecting union views. Whereas before the vote, faculty indicated that the work environment was the most important factor, 4 years later, financial considerations were. Whether this is a result of changing institutional conditions or union experience is unclear.

Based on a survey of more than 500 faculty at three institutions, Graf, Hemmasi, Newgren, and Nielsen (1994) pointed to relationships between hypothetically voting in support of a union and both union sentiment and a set of demographic variables, although they did so with descriptive statistics and ANOVA. Hemmasi and Graf's (1993) use of linear discriminant analysis to consider the same data found that the only nonattitudinal variable to be significant was pay. The strongest predictor was belief in union instrumentality. General union attitudes and liberal political attitudes were also positively related, whereas multiple measures of satisfaction and professionalism were negatively so. These findings fit with the authors' proposed model that the three main determinants of voting behavior are work context, sociopolitical beliefs, and perceived union instrumentality.

Magney (1999) received survey responses from 130 faculty members at Southern Illinois University-Carbondale in the aftermath of a successful organizing drive, addressing questions about voting behaviors in both 1996 and an earlier failed effort. As would be expected, both those who signed union authorization cards and those who voted for bargaining were less satisfied with various aspects of university conditions (teaching and research support, income, faculty influence, and trustworthiness of administrators) than those who did not sign. They also had more positive views of union instrumentality and were far less likely to agree that professional employees should not join unions. Over half of survey respondents who voted yes (52%) indicated that improving faculty governance was the most important factor, followed by compensation issues (20%) and recognition of professional status (11%).

Two other studies from the 1990s examined a different aspect of faculty attitudes but warrant mention here. Through analysis of survey responses from more than 200 faculty at Temple University, McClendon and Klass (1993) and Klass and McClendon (1995) explored correlates of strike-related militancy. In the former, the dependent variables were faculty vote to accept contract offer, vote to reject a court injunction to return to work, and the level of participation in strike actions. The findings confirmed the authors' hypothesis that there were multiple versions of militancy and that contract vote, especially, seemed different than the other two. Only strike instrumentality was significantly correlated with all three outcome variables, whereas union commitment and perceived departmental support of the strike were significant with the latter two. Both discomfort with confrontational militancy and being an instructor or assistant professor were negatively correlated with participation in strike actions. Being in engineering was positively correlated with rejecting the initial contract offer, and overall job satisfaction, organizational commitment, and identifying as female were negatively correlated so, all significantly. Klass and McClendon examined correlates of crossing the picket line at any point during the strike and, for a subsample, during the last 2 days after a court had ordered the faculty back to work. In that analysis, the voting behaviors were among the independent variables, with voting against the strike positively correlating to crossing the picket line in both the full sample and the subsample. Correlations between union commitment and coworker social support with both dependent variables were negative and significant. Satisfaction and perceived hardship were positively correlated with crossing at any point. Significant interaction effects between authorization vote and union commitment, perceived hardship, and social support also existed. Taken together, these two analyses point to the importance of union commitment, instrumentality, satisfaction, social support, and potential costs in different measures of militancy.

At the turn of the century, then, the weight of the evidence pointed to larger social and political views, local work contexts, and views on union and personal efficacy as key factors in predicting faculty attitudes and voting behaviors. Those who believed in unions more broadly, identified as politically liberal, believed that a union could improve conditions, and were dissatisfied with compensation and/or institutional governance were more likely to indicate that they would vote or had voted to collectively bargain. Although some studies still found demographic characteristics such as gender to be predictive, such variables more often proved insignificant in regression analysis.

Lessened Attention in the 21st Century

As with many issues involving faculty unionization, published research studies on the reasons for and attitudes about it have been scant in the 21st century. Goldey, Swank, Hardesty, and Swain (2008) pointed to the lack of recent literature on faculty attitudes and even more so the dearth of studies explicitly considering community colleges. With survey responses from 329 full-time community college faculty members in Kentucky, they undertook stepwise regression ultimately producing four models. In the complete model, the only demographic variable significantly correlated with union attitudes was marital or partnered status, with a weak negative association. More strongly negatively correlated with a prounion attitude was belief in high faculty efficacy in governance and trust in the administration. Participating in a prounion social network, belief in high union efficacy, and political liberalism were all significant in the positive direction. The authors were surprised that socioeconomic class background and several levels of satisfaction including salary, teaching loads, security, and scholarly opportunities were not significant. The results need to be understood in recognition that, contrary to many studies of attitudes, the faculty in this study were at already unionized institutions, potentially changing their networks and information; broader support of unions and real or hypothetical voting behaviors in nonunion environments are potentially different than support in one that is already organized and under contract.

Goeddeke and Kammeyer-Mueller (2010) used a three-part measure of what they called union participation (voting intentions, membership, and card signing) as the dependent variable in their study of more than 300 faculty at a single research university amid an organizing drive. They found that union instrumentality was the strongest predictor of union participation and that "perceived union support" and "perceived organizational support" were equally predictive, but in opposite directions; the former being positive and the latter negative. In their model, the effects of salary, satisfaction, administration and union subjective norms, and general union attitudes were mediated through instrumentality and union/organizational support.

Liao-Troth's (2008) survey of 149 faculty who had participated in union votes at two comprehensive state universities considered nine potential relationships to voting behavior: sense of community, sense of autonomy, trust in management, working environment, career self-efficacy, equity sensitivity, attitudes toward unions, attitudes toward pay, and union activities among peer network. Only attitudes toward unions and peer network were significantly correlated with voting behavior in a regression equation.

Holsinger (2008) relied on broader literature on union attitudes across industries to propose five factors as predictive of voting behavior: favorable attitudes toward unions, union instrumentality, demographic characteristics, work dissatisfaction, and participation in an organizing campaign. Bivariate analysis of surveys of faculty at four points during the organizing campaign at the University of Vermont found all of the nondemographic factors to be significantly related to voting behaviors at each of the four survey points except dissatisfaction with insurance costs, which was at the first and the last. Among demographics, only salary and being a faculty member in the arts and sciences were significant; each was so in all of the survey administrations. Yet when analyzed through logistic regression, few variables were significant at any point. Favoring collective bargaining and being active in organizing were throughout; dissatisfaction with insurance costs was at the last administration and being in arts and sciences was in all but the first survey administration. Pointing to the increased importance of health insurance, Holsinger, himself a union organizer, argued that each campaign has a catalyzing event that can help explain and influence faculty decisions to collectively bargain.

Several recent studies have considered faculty union activism and militancy. Fiorito, Tope, Steinberg, Padavic, and Murphy (2011) found that general satisfaction was negatively related to activism intentions, whereas union longevity and instrumentality were positively related to it at a large public research university. Based on three surveys of faculty at a single research university, Fiorito, Padavic, and Russell (2014) found that prounion attitude, union longevity, and, especially, belief that their activism could make a difference were significantly and positively correlated with activism. In a study of faculty at one institution, Love, Speer, and Buschlen (2015) found financial demands to be the strongest predictor of intent to strike, although views of organizational culture were also significant. As noted previously, however, these issues are somewhat distinct from considerations of voting or union beliefs, and they are treated as such in the larger unionization literature.

Two final recent publications consider faculty attitudes more directly based on data from the 1999–2000 North American Academic Study Survey (NAASS) of full-time faculty at 4-year colleges and universities in Canada and the United States. That phone survey—which included 1,644 U.S. faculty from a range of 4-year institutions and was initially designed by Stanley Rothman, Lipset, Ladd, and Neil Nevitte partly as follow-up to Ladd and Lipset's (1975) *The Divided Academy*—is best known for contested published findings regarding political leanings of college faculty but did include questions about unionization (e.g., Newfield, 2008; Rothman,

Kelly-Woessner, & Woessner, 2011). Rothman, Kelly-Woessner, and Woessner reported that 62% of U.S. faculty surveyed either strongly or moderately agreed that "collective bargaining is important to protect the interests of faculty" (p. 54) with assistant professors (73%) more likely to agree than full professors (52%). Faculty at master's institutions were likewise more likely to agree than those at either baccalaureate or doctoral/research institutions, as were those who indicated that faculty had "little" or "hardly any" input in the institution's governance. Katchanovski, Rothman, and Nevitte (2011) extended the analysis through ordinary least squares regression and reported on three outcome variables from the survey: faculty unions have a divisive effect, collective bargaining has no place in higher education, and collective bargaining is important to protecting faculty interests. In so doing, they flipped the scales on the first two and, somewhat problematically, interpreted a positive correlation on either of the last two as indicative of support for collective bargaining rather than something more specific. Still, their data indicated that being more politically liberal, working at an institution with bargaining, identifying as Black, and identifying as Jewish were positively correlated to a significant degree with the flipped "place of collective bargaining on campus." Household income, administrator opposition, identifying as Asian, identifying as Protestant, and being in the sciences or a "high profession" such as business or engineering were negatively so. They found being politically liberal, the existence of faculty bargaining on campus, a measure of institutional quality, and identifying as Black to be positively correlated with belief in the importance of collective bargaining in protecting faculty interests. Age, household income, identifying as Protestant, being in the sciences, high professions, or other nonhumanities/nonprofessional fields were negatively so. Finally, being politically liberal, socially liberal, and working on a campus with bargaining were positively correlated with the flipped "faculty unions effect," whereas age, income, and being in any field or discipline other than the humanities were negatively so. As two of the very few recent studies to include faculty from multiple institutions, these studies using NAASS data provide some insight, although they are undertheorized and lack methodological and data manipulation details that would make them more useful.

Conclusion

In their review of existing research, Williams and Zirkel (1989) noted "the literature in the field of bargaining seems more concerned with the causes than with the consequences of bargaining" (p. 73). Although the balance of research has shifted in the years since, their larger point remains. Many studies of unionization in higher education, especially those undertaken in the first decade and a half of widespread bargaining in higher education, have sought to ascertain factors associated with faculty decisions to bargain. The vast majority have done so through single institution surveys, many with simple analyses. Barring a few examples, it also remains undertheorized and disproportionally focused on both full-time faculty and 4-year colleges. More work from the great diversity of U.S. higher education and work that attends to the multiple positional types of faculty are needed. So, too, are rigorous considerations that look beyond single or small groups of institutions, especially as most published national studies are either dated or problematic.

What is known fits with what would largely be expected. Early research pointed to demographic characteristics such as age or gender as being related to real or hypothetical voting, though many of these characteristics fell out of later studies that moved beyond bivariate analysis. Compensation issues and general political attitudes were central in early studies, but governance and working condition issues were present as well. In later studies, they became more so. Moreover, measures of satisfaction with and perception of things such as salary appear to be more important than raw numbers. Taken together, then, a combination of broader attitudes about politics and collective bargaining, degrees of satisfaction, views of the faculty's role in governance, and beliefs about the potential efficacy of faculty unions in fostering improvement or causing discord are aligned with reported hypothetical and real voting decisions. So, too, are having peer networks that support unions and being active in organizing oneself. Understanding these characteristics and beliefs can be useful both for those attempting to organize college faculty and those operating at institutions that are in the midst of organizing or bargaining. Of course, each individual case and context is different and larger trends may not hold in specific situations.

Effects of Tenure-Line
Faculty Unions

THE RISE OF widespread collective bargaining in the late 1960s and early 1970s was met not only with excitement and trepidation but also with significant scholarly interest. In addition to the numerous news reports, essays, and opinion pieces issued on the topic, substantial research soon appeared to offer partial answers to questions about the effects of collective bargaining on salaries, governance, collegiality, and other related issues. Some of these were broad-based national studies such as Ladd and Lipset's (1973) famous analysis but many more were focused on local situations and small samples of data. The quantity of this research—if not always the quality—was such that Morand and McPherson (1980) were soon able to comment on "the creation of a new industry—academic studies of academic unionism" (p. 34). By the late 1980s, scholarly publications on the effects of unionization trailed off, especially beyond those appearing in venues specifically tied to collective bargaining in higher education or the public sector. Indeed, it was during this lull that Rhoades (1998) lamented the lack of awareness of faculty unions in the scholarly literature and in higher education graduate programs. It was more than a decade later before the research focus started to rebound amid renewed concerns over the economics of higher education and the roles and rights of faculty in changing institutions. Even then, though, the scholarly attention was less than the topic warrants. It remains so today.

This chapter examines the scholarship on the effects of bargaining by units including tenure-line faculty from the earliest studies at its beginning through the somewhat renewed interest in the topic in the recent past. It does so with an emphasis on the main areas of research—compensation, procedural protections, governance, collegiality, satisfaction, and organizational effectiveness—in largely chronological order, emphasizing the different approaches and findings. Select studies of union contract provisions are included, even though the evidence of union effects provided by them is of a somewhat different nature than most of the studies in the chapter. Taken together, these studies have shown lingering disagreements about the effects of unionization while pointing to the apparent differences in effects by sector. They have also highlighted the difficulties in accurately capturing the effects of unionization, including its local and contextual nature, temporal changes, and methodological challenges. Moreover, the threat to unionize has the potential to foster changes, which could mitigate the apparent effects of actually unionizing, as could broader labor market pressures. As such, although the larger finding is of generally positive or neutral effects for faculty, much is left unknown.

Compensation

With the traditional association of unionization with wages and benefits, it is unsurprising that more studies of the effects of faculty bargaining have focused on compensation than any other issue. Early considerations of faculty unionization looked at bargaining agreements in a handful of institutions and systems, pointing to equity issues and questioning whether incremental increases would have occurred without the unions. Though focused on governance, Mortimer and Lozier (1972) noted an emphasis on set salary schedules and pay equity over merit pay in their study of 31 bargained contracts. Ladd and Lipset (1973), acknowledging that faculty unionization was too recent a phenomenon to accurately gauge its effects, pointed to slight differences in individual contracts but consistent evidence of privileging the leveling of salaries within ranks over merit pay. They further noted the difficulty in assessing whether bargained salary increases were a result of specific contracts or might have otherwise been gained.

Carr and Van Eyck (1973) considered this difficulty more fully, noting the early appearance of a wage premium for unions at community colleges and suggesting that it might be based on the close ties between institutions in that sector and recently unionized K–12 systems. The evidence for such a premium at 4-year institutions was not as clear. Faculty in the City University of New York (CUNY) received substantial raises in their 1969 union contract, but administrators claimed that they would have received them regardless of the contract—CUNY wages were pinned to K–12 wages in the city, which had increased substantially because of teacher union bargaining. Bargained raises in the State University of New York (SUNY) system were on par with those of state civil service workers, but the faculty union contract at Central Michigan University provided "one of the strongest cases" (p. 245) for increased compensation at a 4-year institution, though the union and institution offered competing claims as to the actual percentage increase in total compensation. Indeed, throughout, Carr and Van Eyck pointed to the challenges in assessing overall compensation rather than the more straightforward salary and the difficulty in evaluating the claims of participants in bargaining.

Union–Nonunion Wage and Compensation Differentials

Literature on union–nonunion wage and compensation differentials is more widely available than that on many issues, though remains somewhat unfulfilling. Early studies pairing unionized and nonunionized institutions were replaced by those that used more robust methods and national-level data, including from NCES. Some of this work is quite useful, though the most robust relies on data that are now more than a decade old.

Matching Studies and Their Critics. Birnbaum's (1974, 1976) studies of the effects of bargaining on faculty compensation initiated the approach that would dominate for the rest of the decade: matching unionized and nonunionized institutions and examining changes in compensation over time through descriptive and basic statistics. Using AAUP survey data and 1968–1969 as a baseline, Birnbaum (1974) considered total compensation at 88 pairs of institutions matched by control, level, base-year compensation, faculty size, and location. When analyzed together, he found statistically significant differences in compensation in the direction of greater increases for bargaining faculty. When analyzed in four groups based on institutional type, only at public universities and public 4-year colleges did they reach significance. Birnbaum cautioned that a possible explanation could have been the broader context of state employee bargaining, with faculty receiving spillover benefits, but interpreted the results as demonstrating the potential benefits of unionizing for faculty. For Birnbaum, the results were remarkable considering that many of the unionized institutions had been recognized for high compensation even before bargaining.

Birnbaum's (1976) follow-up study of 59 institutional pairs based on 1974–1975 data offered slightly different findings. Although confirming that unionized faculty maintained larger overall salary increases than nonunionized in paired institutions, the differences narrowed. Overall, the salary differences when compared to 1968–1969 remained significant, though the differences between 1972–1973 and 1974–1975 were not. Statistically significant differences were again found for public universities and public 4-year colleges, with the latter also showing significant changes from 1972–1973 to 1974–1975. In this analysis, private colleges and universities also showed significant differences (though only at the .05 level) in salary increases favoring unionized faculty since 1968–1969. At paired community colleges, unionized faculty saw greater increases than nonunionized but not significantly so. Moreover, nonunionized institutions saw greater increases than unionized between 1972–1973 and 1974–1975. Birnbaum reasoned that such findings suggested that his earlier conclusions about the positive effects of bargaining on salaries needed to be reconsidered; unions may not have been as powerful as he had suggested, as institutional, state, and economic conditions might prove more important. It is also conceivable that what Birnbaum found was a spillover effect where the nonunionized faculty were benefiting from the actions of their unionized peers.

Staller (1975) created a compensation model for community college faculty, attempting to account for full-time equivalent enrollment, student-to-faculty ratio, average starting public school salary of teachers with a master's degree, unionization, and other issues. With 1970–1971 data about 263 community colleges, he found salary to be unrelated to unionization but both fringe benefits and total compensation to be significantly positively related.

Much of the work for the next few years, though, either pursued matching techniques or explicitly challenged them. Aussieker (1975a) undertook three small comparisons of faculty salaries at unionized and nonunionized 2-year institutions, finding insignificant differences when factoring in cost of living (COL). However, he cautioned that the quality of data and the larger contexts made any conclusions suspect. Morgan and Kearney (1977) paired 46 four-year institutions, using regression to examine both faculty compensation and change in compensation from 1969–1970 to 1974–1975. They found unionization to be significantly associated with higher compensation when a number of institutional and state-level characteristics were held equal; when disaggregated by institutional type, the data "suggest[ed] that the gains in compensation among collectivized campuses have come among faculties at the less comprehensive institutions" (p. 32).

These matching studies, especially that by Morgan and Kearney (1977), were harshly critiqued by Brown and Stone (1977b, 1977c), who found findings unsubstantiated, matches problematic, and the different starting points for contracts troublesome. Perhaps most important, Brown and Stone (1977b) identified a temporal problem—though unionized, some of Morgan and Kearney's institutions had not yet successfully negotiated a contract by 1974–1975 so the effects of bargaining on 1974–1975 salaries were, at best, suspect. Indeed, the critique actually understated the concern as some of the unionized institutions in the sample that had achieved contracts were statutorily prohibited from bargaining on compensation.

Brown and Stone (1977a) offered their own comparison of salaries and compensation at 37 unionized institutions to national and regional averages, both before and after unionization. They found that unionized institutions did not exhibit lower salaries or compensation prior to bargaining and that, at the instructor and assistant professor ranks, there were no significant differences in salary growth. Statistically significant differences in the direction of greater growth for unionized associate and full professors were found but were attributed largely to conditions at five Pennsylvania campuses that they viewed as having unique characteristics. Removing these campuses, while also excluding New York City institutions, removed any significance. Leslie and

Hu (1977), however, suggested that the variables used, including national and regional averages, limited the appropriateness of the conclusion.

Arguing that Kearney and Morgan (1977) had successfully countered the critiques of their work, Ito and Masoner (1980) reexamined Brown and Stone's (1977a) sample based on bargaining unit (which could include multiple campuses), rather than campus, a substantial change as roughly two thirds of the campuses in Brown and Stone's study were part of five larger systems. Applying Brown and Stone's methods at the institutional level ending in 1974–1975—the last year of data in Morgan and Kearney's (1977) study—Ito and Masoner found a statistically significant positive relationship between unionization and salary growth. When extended the additional year that Brown and Stone (1977a) included, the significance disappeared. Ito and Masoner speculated that this might reflect the financial difficulties of the examined region, as much as unionization more broadly. Still, they agreed that there appeared to have been a fall-off in the association of unions and salary growth. Birnbaum's (1977) reanalysis of the institutions he had studied found a curvilinear trend from small wage differences in the first 2 years, to larger ones in the next four, back to smaller and then almost no differences. The multiple findings pointed to the inherent difficulty in studying the effects of bargaining on faculty salaries and the instability of gains amid broader economic changes.

Leslie and Hu (1977) argued that Morgan and Kearney's (1977) study was the most methodologically advanced to date, building on the best part of both Birnbaum's (1974, 1976) and Brown and Stone (1977a). They pursued similar methods in their analysis of 150 pairs of 2- and 4-year institutions, considering change in compensation from 1969–1970 to 1975–1976 while also examining institutional income and expenditures to determine if there were relationships to unionization. They found unionization correlated with increased government appropriations and increased student tuition and fees, the latter suggesting that students were being charged more to account for greater faculty compensation. More central to this discussion, they found that the salary benefits of unionization had shrunk but that they remained significant, although accruing only to associate and full professors. At the 4-year institutions, compensation benefits were largest at the least prestigious and private institutions, though the gap between public and private was narrow compared to the Morgan and Kearney (1977) findings. At 2-year institutions, the gap had all but disappeared. These results again suggested that there might be a leveling-off effect, wherein initial bargaining gains are difficult to sustain.

Marshall's (1979) study of 30 matched pairs of 2- and 4-year institutions found no differences in salaries in AAUP category I and II institutions, positive effects of unionization at AAUP category III institutions, and negative effects at 2-year institutions, contributing to the growing sense that the effects of unionization on salaries might not be lasting. At the same time, Marshall raised the concern that the findings in all of these studies might have been "methodological artifacts" (p. 319) tied to the pairings used and the analyses undertaken. The following year, though, Morand and McPherson (1980) raised a more basic concern: they claimed that the AAUP data underlying all of these analyses were fundamentally flawed.

Still, the same basic approaches were continued into the 1980s. Guthrie-Morse, Leslie, and Hu (1981) returned to 30 pairs of 4-year institutions from Leslie and Hu's (1977) study, extending the data to 1977–1978. In so doing, they found that 1974–1975 appeared to be the high point in unionized faculty compensation premiums; when accounting for COL, the union premiums had since disappeared. The work confirmed earlier studies that compensation gains were greatest at the least complex institutions but complicated findings that full and associate professors benefited the most. They found those advantages declined over time and, just as important, by disaggregating untenured faculty into assistant professors and instructors, they found the latter group benefited as well. In an article published the following year but relying on older data, Hu and Leslie (1982) again examined paired institutions and again found compensation premiums for faculty that disappeared and were even negative when regional COL was considered. Baker (1984a, 1984b) likewise found no significant long-term wage premiums, although there were some short-term gains.

Nearly a decade later, Wiley (1993) returned to matching as one technique in her study of community college salaries in California. She found that unionization was not a significant predictor of faculty salaries. By that time, though, scholars had largely abandoned matching techniques because of the concerns that had been articulated by Brown and Stone (1977b, 1977c) and the possibilities that both new data and techniques offered. Taken together, the matched paired studies were inconclusive. Most showed some association between unionization and faculty gains in compensation, though the results were stronger in the short term than in the long term. Moreover, when COL was included in the analyses, many of the findings of premiums vanish.

Beyond Matching Debates. As Brown and Stone's (1977a) research and Ito and Masoner's (1981) reconsideration of it highlighted, not all of the work undertaken in the 1970s used matching techniques; even less did in subsequent decades. In a study that Bacharach, Schmidle, and Bauer (1987) would term "the most comprehensive investigation of collective bargaining's impact on faculty pay" (p. 249), Freeman (1978) examined AAUP data from 1965 to 1976, both cross-sectionally and using a fixed effects model. Both techniques yielded evidence that unionization was linked to increased compensation, with those institutions that organized early demonstrating larger increases. Freeman found that the differences in fringe benefits were greater than those in salary and that unionized full professors saw larger differentials than those at other ranks. Importantly, he found that changing the base year of compensation changed the results, with a substantially larger effect with 1965 as the starting point than with 1970. To Freeman, this was fitting with the confusion in the existing literature and pointed to the need for better sampling and techniques.

Based on 1985–1986 data, Jackson and Clark (1987) examined salaries and compensation at 4-year institutions, including a range of institutional characteristics as independent variables. In the full model, collective bargaining was a significant predictor of both salary and compensation, though with less explanatory importance than measures of size, credentials, selectivity, institutional revenues, and private secular type. When public and private institutions were examined separately, collective bargaining remained positive and significant in public but not private institutions. Others focused more narrowly on the sector of higher education least likely to unionize: doctoral granting and research universities. Using 1981 AAUP data and including numerous faculty, institutional, and geographical variables, Kesselring (1991) found that unionized faculty at PhD-granting institutions earned substantially less than nonunionized faculty, although the lower salaries might have been the cause of unionization rather than an effect. Browne and Trieschmann (1991) examined only full professors and found insignificant negative relationships between unionization and benefit compensation. Smith (1992) found significant salary premiums for full and associate professors but not assistant professors. She did not, however, offer any controls for COL or other potentially relevant factors.

Building upon Freeman's (1978) work and considering a variety of institutional characteristics (e.g., faculty size, faculty credentials, student–faculty ratio, selectivity, location, control, type), Rees (1993) estimated a union–nonunion compensation differential of 4% to 7% based on cross-sectional analysis of AAUP data from the mid-1980s. He also found that unions affiliated with more than one national organization saw the greatest salary premiums, whereas those with the AAUP saw the smallest. Years organized had an unexplained "peculiar" (p. 408) relationship to compensation with initial positive relationship, followed by reductions for 6 to 8 years and then surges. He found no differences between public and private institutions but greater differentials at 2-year colleges than 4. Rees' fixed effects model using data from 1970–1971 to 1987–1988 and controlling for type, faculty size, year, and percentages of faculty at different ranks told a different story—unionization was associated with a statistically significant reduction in compensation. As such, he concluded that the "research casts doubt on the existence of a positive union-nonunion differential" (p. 417).

In the late-1980s, scholars began looking beyond AAUP and Higher Education General Information Survey data, which had served as the basis for most early studies. Barbezat (1989), for example, relied on Ladd and Lipset's (1978) 1977 Survey of the American Professoriate, which itself faced criticism over design (Lang, 1981). With 3,404 faculty members at 158 institutions in her final dataset and measures of both individual (e.g., rank, seniority, race, and research productivity) and institutional (e.g., type, and region) characteristics as independent variables, Barbezat estimated a salary advantage for unionized faculty at under 2%. She further found that unionization correlated with higher salary for more senior faculty, with small increases for article publication and small differentials across disciplines. Ashraf's (1992) analysis of data from 2,988 faculty from the same dataset with slightly different controls resulted in somewhat different findings: 4.4% salary differentials for unionized faculty overall, but with a wide range from −7.63% to +13.07%, depending on the subgrouping. The salary benefits for unionized faculty were higher at higher ranks. Ashraf (1997) would later say that the results of his and Barbezat's work aligned, but the differences in their results were another indication of the difficulties in assessing the effects of bargaining.

Studies Using National Center for Education Statistics Data. The National Study of Postsecondary Faculty (NSOPF), first undertaken in 1987–1988 by the U.S. Department of Education's NCES, offered new possibilities for studying salaries, though not total compensation. Lillydahl and Singell (1993) examined the salaries of full-time faculty in the arts and sciences in 4-year institutions by rank. Controlling for institutional measures, faculty productivity, individual characteristics, and satisfaction, they found that full and associate professors had positive significant salary differentials at unionized institutions but that assistant professors had insignificant negative differentials. They estimated that, holding other things constant, unionized full and associate professors had 13.2% and 6.4% higher salaries, respectively, than nonunionized peers. To the authors, these results suggested that unionization helped counter salary compression. Importantly, institutional type mattered, with unionized faculty having a significant lower salary at research universities than nonunionized faculty.

In an effort to update his (1992) and Barbezat's (1989) work, Ashraf (1997) used 1988 NSOPF data along with that from the 1969 Carnegie Council National Survey of Higher Education and the 1977 Survey of the American Professoriate. He concluded that a negative union premium existed in 1969 but that small but significant positive premiums did in 1977 and 1989. The union premiums that did exist were highest at comprehensive colleges, with negative premiums at research and doctoral institutions in 1977 and, even more so, 1989. Unionization aligned with smaller gender and race wage differentials and smaller benefits to senior faculty. Using 1993 NSOPF data, Ashraf (1998) considered wage premiums at specific institutional types finding wage premiums to be largest at community colleges (8.43%), to be positive at comprehensive universities (2.42%), and to be negative at doctoral and research universities (−2.67%). Overall, he found a marginally negative (−0.44%) union–nonunion wage difference.

Monks (2000) criticized Ashraf's (1998) study for not accounting for substantial numbers of non-tenure-line faculty and the oversampling of some disciplines in the survey. Using a subset of 1993 NSOPF data and accounting for additional institutional and individual characteristics, he estimated that unionized faculty earned between 7% and 14% more than nonunionized faculty, depending on the specifications used. Like Ashraf, he found less dispersion in salaries across disciplines among unionized institutions and low effects of publications. Although noting that the preponderance of unions at public and 2-year institutions made cross-type considerations risky, Monks argued that previous research appeared to underestimate the union wage premium, though Hedrick, Henson, Krieg, and Wassell (2011) later questioned the large number of 2-year institutions in his sample.

Using the 1993 NSOPF data with additional controls for discipline and public–private control, Ashraf (1999) found a positive union premium at public comprehensive universities but negative premiums at private comprehensives and both public and private research and doctoral universities. In an update, using 1999 NSOPF data, Ashraf and Williams (2008) found a positive overall union wage differential (1.08%), with positive differentials at private universities (1.57%), public comprehensive universities (3.51%), and private comprehensive universities (5.50%). Also based on 1999 NSOPF data, Schuster and Finkelstein (2006) likewise argued that a union wage premium existed for most academic fields but appeared especially prominent in the humanities and other fields with relatively lower demand. Using 2004 NSOPF data, Ashraf and Aydin (2009) found a 5.18% union premium for all faculty but again with great variations. No significance was found at research or doctoral universities, but significant positive relationships were found at comprehensive universities (8.16%), liberal arts colleges (3.71%), and 2-year colleges (10.89%). Using 2011–2012 AAUP data, Finkelstein, Conley, and Schuster (2016) found similar differences by type. Yet although the authors in many of these studies controlled for certain institutional or disciplinary characteristics, other potentially important ones were missing. Moreover, their narrow focus on salaries offered only partial evidence of compensation, a crucial factor as some authors have argued that faculty unions might be more successful in affecting benefits than wages. As Shuster and Finkelstein (2006) noted in qualifying their findings, "it is challenging to isolate the effects of collective bargaining on faculty salaries" (p. 261) and "generalizations must yield to more complex analyses" (p. 262).

More complex analyses were undertaken by Hedrick et al. (2011) and Henson, Krieg, Wassell, and Hedrick (2012), who in related studies reexamined unionization and salaries using NSOPF data from 1988, 1993, 1999, and 2004. Noting the findings of Guthrie-Morse et al. (1981) and Hu and Leslie (1982), the authors of these studies were particularly concerned that recent work had ignored COL, thus rendering their results questionable. Moreover, the authors included institution-specific factors other studies had not otherwise attempted to correct previous shortcomings. Examining faculty at 4-year institutions, Hedrick et al. found no union wage premium, although they maintained that unions could still offer other benefits. Henson, et al. (2012) applied the techniques and additional variables to 2-year institutions, resulting in much smaller estimates of union wage premiums than had appeared in Rees (1993) and Ashraf (1998): 2.8% for basic salary and 3.0% for a salary measure including supplementary wages paid by the institution for activities such as summer teaching. Although they acknowledged the possibility of underestimating and of spillover effects, these authors provided substantial evidence that union wage premiums may have previously been overstated.

Other researchers looked beyond NSOPF data, including Benedict (2007), who sought to reexamine public sector union wage premiums from 1978–1985 and 1989–1996 using NCES institution-level data in conjunction with that of union contracts and school classifications. With variables for institutional characteristics (e.g., percent tenured, percent female, enrollment, student–faculty ratio, type, tuition, revenues), Benedict found a union wage premium of 5% in the earlier period and 13% in the latter. Her data, though, were devoid of individual characteristics and she did not account for COL. Finally, two recent studies returned to ideas underpinning some of the earliest pairing studies—that finding the appropriate comparison groups is central to understanding the relationships between faculty salaries and unionization. Mayhall, Katsinas, and Bray (2015) argued that studies of 2-year colleges were hampered by the variations in 2-year colleges related to local appropriations and geographic type. Using 2010–2011 NCES Human Resource Survey data, geographic type information from the Carnegie Classification system, and appropriations information from Grapevine, they found that full-time faculty with collective bargaining agreements earned more in total compensation than those without in each of the seven categories of type (rural small, medium, and large; suburban and urban and single and multicampus). Katsinas, Ogun, and Bray (2016) likewise argued that geography was important in their study of regional universities, which they contended constitute a distinct type that needs to be analyzed as such. Using similar data from 2010–2011, they found positive differences for unionized faculty in terms of both salaries and fringe benefits in each of their seven categories, many of which appear substantial, though without controls for COL beyond what might be suggested by urbanicity.

Summary of Research on Wage and Compensation Premiums. Taken together, the studies of bargaining and salary/compensation are ultimately unsatisfying. Many studies have been hampered by concerns about data, including the accuracy of that which have been collected and its robustness for the questions being examined. Some have been limited by the lack of individual-level data, potentially obscuring important factors in faculty salaries. Moreover, temporal issues are extremely important as short-term economic factors can fundamentally affect bargaining (e.g., Hicks, 2014). Contracts negotiated in those periods might appear to offer little gains but could actually provide more than what would have otherwise been had. Spillover effects and compensation gains related to efforts to forestall unionization may also blur the picture; as might situations such as that pointed out by Begin (1979) based on work by Bain (1976) and Garbarino (1975): significant wage gains at unionized institutions in New York and New Jersey were based on policies linking faculty salaries to those of K–12 teachers and other public sector workers, not necessarily *faculty* union efforts. The particulars of state law and policy are significant but often missing considerations. Perhaps most important, studies that do not in some way account for differences in COL are problematic, especially as early unionization often took place in states with higher COL. Of course, even the studies that offer the best evidence cannot make causal claims.

Although many early studies of unionization pointed to a wage or compensation premium in 4-year colleges, especially for senior faculty at comprehensive colleges, Hedrick et al.'s (2011) study suggested that there is not a statistically significant difference in pay across 4-year institutions. In 2-year institutions, the weight of the evidence points to a union wage premium, though if Henson et al.'s (2012) findings are correct, it is smaller than many had previously assumed. Still, the diversity in findings, changes over time, and difficulties in measurement leave the question somewhat unsettled.

Merit, Pay Leveling, and Equity

Many of the studies discussed here included considerations beyond union–nonunion wage differentials, including potentially different premiums by rank and the effects of unionization on differentials by faculty characteristics. In his work just as bargaining was catching hold, Garbarino (1972) proposed that faculty unionization appeared to offer the greatest benefits to the most junior and underserved faculty. Pointing to evidence from case studies of five unionized institutions, he argued, "The paradox of faculty unionism to date is that the greatest gains have accrued to the teaching faculty on the margin of the core faculty, to the faculty of the institutions in the integrated systems that have been lowest in the academic hierarchy, and to the non-faculty professionals" (p. 15). These gains included salary leveling as well as increased security. Yet Carr and Van Eyck (1973) questioned this interpretation, noting "experience with faculty collective bargaining does not yet provide overwhelming evidence of a leveling, homogenizing effect on faculty salaries" (p. 267). Indeed, as noted previously, many ensuing studies found that bargaining most benefitted the senior members of the faculty over the junior (e.g., Ashraf, 1992; Barbezat, 1989; Hu & Leslie, 1982; Leslie & Hu, 1977; Lillydahl & Singell, 1993; Smith, 1992), whereas a number of studies found no difference or mixed results (e.g., Baker, 1984a; Brown & Stone, 1977a; Marshall, 1979). Rarer were studies such as Guthrie-Morse et al.'s (1981), which pointed to superior union wage premiums for assistant professors and/or instructors. That finding might be explained by the relative decline in merit pay provisions in the unionized institutions that they included in their study.

A handful of studies have focused more directly on dispersion. White's (1982) case study of state universities in Minnesota (excepting the University of Minnesota) drew from median voter theory to examine if the returns on bargaining would be greatest for the average worker. Comparing the percentage of total wages in the 1978–1979 contract to both that proposed by the union and the final agreed-upon contract in 1980–1981, he argued that it was the assistant and associate professors, not instructors or full professors, who benefited the most from the new contract. Duncan, Krall, Maxcy, and Prus's (2004) study of faculty seniority at a public liberal arts college noted that unionization did not always aid the most senior faculty cohorts, as negotiated across-the-board adjustments failed to counter existing compression.

A subset of these studies have considered contract provisions as related to salary structures and/or equity, including Bognanno, Estenson, and Suntrup's (1978) finding that only 9% of the 59 contracts examined had equalization clauses, whereas 27% had a formula for equalization and percentage increases. Fifteen percent had salary scales based on rank and seniority, and slightly fewer than half had provisions for merit raises; only one precluded merit pay. Johnstone's (1981) examination of 89 four-year institution contracts found that 36% included provisions for merit pay; 91% of the most prestigious institutions did. Only 25% included provisions for equity adjustments, some of which were combined with merit provisions. In a broader sample of close to 200 contracts, Douglas and Goldsmith (1981, as cited by Hansen, 1988) found only 17% with merit pay provisions.

Hansen (1988) pointed to the vague nature and variety of merit pay approaches in contracts before noting that 48% of the AAUP contracts he analyzed included some form, mostly as a one-time bonus. Rhoades's (1998) consideration of 203 contracts found that merit provisions were more common than equity or market adjustment provisions, appearing in 48 contracts compared with 26 and 21, respectively. The majority of 4-year contracts included merit provisions, though few 2-year contracts did. More 4-year than 2-year included both equity and market adjustment language. He concluded that the across-the-board increases helped to mitigate further disciplinary dispersion of salaries although they did nothing to upend it. Moreover, administrators retained significant discretion as contracts included provisions for exceptions to the salary schedule; at one, 25% of all faculty could be excepted from it.

Wassell, Hedrick, Henson, and Krieg (2015) examined wage distribution in another way, using NSOPF data to examine more than 24,000 faculty in 25 academic fields at 1,060 institutions. When controlling for COL, experience, rank, productivity, and other variables, they found substantial and significant differences in union wage benefits across fields. This "flattening" of salaries was most pronounced at comprehensive institutions but also occurred at doctoral institutions. It was least likely at liberal arts colleges. Moreover, although there was no statistically significant increase in average wage, there were gains at the median salary level as the distribution of expected gains was skewed positively.

Union advocates have argued that unions have the potential to counteract gender-based salary inequities (e.g., Curtis, 2011) but the evidence is, again, inconsistent. In her study of doctoral institutions, Smith (1992) found male–female wage gaps at all three ladder ranks at both unionized and nonunionized institutions. She found slightly smaller gaps at unionized institutions, which she suggested demonstrated a union benefit. In a later version of the study using 2007–2008 data from the Integrated Postsecondary Education Data System, Smith and Grosso (2009) found the gender wage gap to be larger at all ranks in unionized institutions. In a more advanced study, based on 1994–1995 AAUP data on 1,120 four-year institutions, Sosin, Rives, and West (1998) found that women at both unionized and nonunionized institutions earned less at each rank than men and did so at each of four institutional types. Only at the assistant level did they find clear differences in union–nonunion gender wage differentials, estimating a $734 benefit per year for unionized women. There was no apparent benefit for associate professors and the findings for full professors were mixed. They concluded, "Unions matter, but not to an extent that is likely to be considered satisfactory by the unions or by women" (p. 40). Perhaps this can be explained by Rhoades's (1998) finding that gender did "not figure prominently" (p. 260) in the contracts he examined.

Beliefs About and Satisfaction with Compensation

A subset of studies that deal with compensation have considered how satisfied faculty are with their salaries and the effect that institutional stakeholders believe that the union has had. These are important considerations as satisfaction with salary is often linked to views on unionization, as is discussed in the third chapter. Hedgepeth's (1974) study of unionization at SUNY Cortland found concern about the negative consequences of unionization on salaries and a belief that salary increments had been lost through the process, with corresponding low morale and concerns about the institution's ability to recruit and retain faculty. Faculty were likewise concerned both about continuing pay inequities and an unclear merit pay process. On the other hand, based on their 1979 survey and additional research, Baldridge, Kemerer, and Associates (1981) noted that all parties admitted some benefits for unionized faculty in terms of wages and benefits, with union presidents arguing that they were far more substantial than university officials.

In his study of more than 1,000 unionized and nonunionized faculty in Pennsylvania, Hill (1982) found the most pronounced differences in satisfaction occurring in the economic dimension, with unionized faculty being significantly more highly satisfied. As noted, however, Brown and Stone (1977a) argued that unionized institutions in Pennsylvania saw unusually large rises in salary in the 1970s, which may or may not have been a result of unionization. Gomez-Mejia and Balkin (1984) considered satisfaction at two paired statewide systems, one unionized (Minnesota) and one not (Wisconsin). They found unionized faculty to be significantly more satisfied with their salaries when other determinants of satisfaction were controlled, including level of pay. They further found that women in the unionized system were more satisfied with pay than men, but that there were no differences in the nonunionized system, suggesting that there might be equity benefits of unionizing. Balkin (1989) matched two public doctoral granting institutions in the southeast and surveyed a total of 295 faculty, finding union members were significantly more satisfied with their benefits than nonunion members but not so on three other measures of compensation, including salary. The limited scope of the study, though, raises concerns about broader applicability.

Ormsby and Ormsby (1988) examined satisfaction longitudinally based on pre- and postunionization surveys of 90 faculty members at a single metropolitan university. In their study, like that of Gomez-Mejia and Balkin (1984), the only significant difference in five areas of satisfaction was in salary. Finley (1991) surveyed a total of 222 faculty at 10 matched pairs of 2-year institutions, finding a small but not statistically significant positive difference in economic satisfaction for unionized faculty. Eight other dimensions saw a negative difference, with three being statistically significant (governance, support, and convenience).

Elmuti and Kathawala's (1991) survey of 294 faculty members at a unionized university in rural Illinois revealed only one third of the respondents believed the union had a positive effect on compensation, with older tenured men being least likely and younger tenured women being most likely to believe in a positive effect. The authors pointed to salary inversion as a possible cause. Follow-up interviews revealed some misunderstandings of the union's characteristics and frustration with the inability to personally negotiate salaries, as well as the belief that the most useful role of the union was in providing a collective voice to the administration, the governing board, and the state. Dallinger and Beveridge (1993) replicated the study at a comprehensive university operating under the same bargaining contract. They found largely consistent results, although with slightly less satisfaction with the union, including in compensation. Lillydahl and Singell's (1993) aforementioned study of faculty at 4-year colleges included the finding that unionized faculty were significantly more satisfied with pay and benefits than nonunionized, but that nonunionized faculty were more satisfied overall. This suggests a trading of benefits or that the conditions that relate to unionization might relate to satisfaction.

Studies of faculty union job satisfaction tailed off after the Dallinger and Beveredge (1993) and Lillydahl and Singell (1993) studies, as did much of the research on unionization, only returning more than a decade later. Even then most studies focused on other factors related to union satisfaction, with Krieg, Wassell, Hedrick, and Henson (2013) standing out as an exception. Like Lillydahl and Singell, they used NSOPF data to consider multiple aspects of satisfaction at 4-year institutions. They found unionized tenure-line faculty to be significantly more satisfied with their total compensation, though not overall more satisfied. Considering Hedrick et al.'s (2011) finding of no wage premium at 4-year colleges and universities, they suggested that this was because of a perception of bargaining effect more than an actual effect.

Overall, the evidence is somewhat mixed and much of it is dated. Most of the studies were localized in specific institutions or contexts, lacking both generalizability and enough detail to provide confidence that the findings might apply broadly. At the same time, the weight of the evidence, including that provided by the Krieg et al. (2013), indicates that tenure-line faculty operating under bargained contracts are more satisfied with their compensation than those who are not operating as such.

Overview of Research on Compensation

In sum, then, the effects of collective bargaining on issues related to compensation are among the most studied aspects of faculty unionization though the findings are not as clear and consistent as might be preferred. Evidence suggests, but only suggests, that unionization may be linked with short-term gains in certain contexts and environments that might also differ by institutional type. The most recent evidence questions whether a union wage premium exists at 4-year colleges, though that is a large and diverse group that, as Katsinas et al. (2016) have argued, needs to be disaggregated and studied further. It appears that to the extent that they exist, they are more likely at comprehensive and baccalaureate institutions than at research universities. Moreover, salary is only one aspect of compensation and, as then-AAUP president Cary Nelson (2011) suggested, even without a salary premium, there could be a compensation one. There is more evidence of both at 2-year institutions. Some have found a flattening of salaries and increased equity, but others have noted that entrenched disparities have been negotiated into contracts. The research does suggest that unionized faculty are more satisfied with their remuneration than nonunionized, despite uncertainty as to whether bargaining helped. As Rhoades and Torres-Olave (2015) noted while highlighting the shortcomings in our understandings, we "know relatively little about the salary issues studied at the inception of faculty unionization, about the extent to which there is a positive impact of unionization on salaries and benefits, and about whether there are spillover effects of union wages and benefits to nonunionized setting" (p. 420).

Tenure, Grievance Procedures, and Retrenchment Policies

Compensation is, of course, only one of many areas on which unions focus their efforts and might have an impact. Job security and procedural protections are another key area of potential influence; for some, they are every bit as or more important than wages and benefits. As is outlined in the third chapter and discussed elsewhere in the literature (e.g., DeCew, 2003; Wickens, 2008), issues related to job security, tenure, and due process can influence decisions to unionize and can be key goals for bargaining. A number of studies have examined aspects related to tenure, promotion, and procedural protections, though not nearly as many as have considered wages and benefits. Taken together, they show a formalization of procedures for achieving tenure, increased procedural protections and grievance policies, and uneven results in retrenchment policies.

Formalized Procedures

Ladd and Lipset (1973) emphasized the debates over tenure procedures and rates, juxtaposing worries about academic quality with concerns for equity and protection from arbitrary decisions. They argued that faculty unions had sought to extend tenure rights, formalize procedures, and create appeal processes for those who were denied tenure, emphasizing "humane treatment" (p. 75) of probationary faculty who could be terminated rather than tenured without ever receiving a negative review of their work. Ultimately, they agreed with Garbarino's (1972) contention that "among regular rank faculty, the most significant benefits have accrued to a relatively small fraction of the junior faculty who have improved their chances of continuing employment in a weak labor market" (p. 3).

In writings from their national study, Kemerer and Baldridge (e.g., 1975; 1975–1976) likewise highlighted the tensions between security and protectionism, noting that the latter could favor seniority and mediocrity over merit. Still, they found little evidence that tenure by default was occurring because of unionization. They further argued that unions had,

> *made impressive progress in affecting personnel policies. Basic issues of hiring, firing, promotion, and tenure are usually included in initial union contracts.... Probably their most positive function is to support reasonable and fair personnel practices in institutions weak in those areas. (1975–1976, p. 50)*

Other early studies similarly pointed to the inclusion of personnel policies as a key development in bargaining, even if they were not included in all contracts (e.g., Goodwin & Andes, 1972; Mortimer & Lozier, 1973). Hedgepeth's (1974) case study of SUNY highlighted concern that the formalized procedures brought about by bargaining could be time consuming and that it was too early to tell the benefits of grievance procedures but that their very establishment was a positive.

In his review of research and analysis of 31 contracts, Mortimer (1974) noted the inclusion of tenure provisions in contracts (80% in his sample) and highlighted that some of those without explicit policies still spoke to tenure through references to other institutional policies or state law. He and others (e.g., Ladd & Lipset, 1973) linked grievance procedures and arbitration to tenure policies, as negative decisions were the primary causes of grievance filings at CUNY and SUNY. Of those contracts that included explicit mention of tenure, slightly more than half included provisions for binding arbitration of appealed tenure decisions, whereas most others included some other form of appeal process. Mortimer warned that some contract provisions might decouple academic freedom and tenure, and instead link the latter more closely with job security, including in times of retrenchment. Yet, he concluded, "These data raise as many questions as they answer" (p. 7).

Some early work focused more explicitly on due process and grievance procedures both in relation to tenure decisions and more broadly. These procedures were, according to Johnstone (1981), "essentially universal" in higher education contracts, though with variation across institutions. Leslie's (1975) study of conflict management relied on data from more 200 unionized and nonunionized institutions, including paired matches of 17 unionized and 17 nonunionized institutions. Based on contract analysis and other information, he found that bargained grievance procedures emphasized contract enforcement, whereas nonbargained ones covered a broader array of issues. He also concluded that contract grievance procedures were more complex; that peer review had a greater, though not decisive role in noncontract procedures; and that procedures and usage differed by sector but bargained grievance procedures were more often used. Kemerer and Baldridge (1975) likewise noted that bargained grievance procedures could be heavily relied upon and warned that arbitration might not be a good fit for higher education. Upon further analysis of additional data, however, Baldridge, Kemerer, and Associates (1981) changed course, noting that some of their worries had been unfounded. Contractual language had improved in ways that protected peer review while allowing arbitrators to decide on procedural issues or potentially arbitrary rulings. Administrators remained concerned but, largely, bargaining and arbitration made personnel decisions "more rational and fair" (p. 42). This finding—that grievance procedures could be positive, did not necessarily cause strife, and would not necessarily be overused—mirrored Begin's (1977) findings in his study of Rutgers University.

In her review of the existing literature, Lee (1978) concluded that tenure rights had been firmly established through their inclusion in union contracts. The argument received further support from a 1979 College and University Personnel Association (CUPA) survey, which found that 88% of unionized campuses had written tenure policies, whereas only 55% of nonunionized campuses did (Baldridge et al., 1981). Building on the CUPA data, Baldridge et al. (1981) argued that unionization seemed to make the most difference in community colleges and private institutions. In the former, tenure systems of any kind were far more likely at unionized institutions than nonunionized ones. In the latter, formalized tenure procedures were far more likely at unionized institutions. Guthrie-Morse et al. (1981) added that there was a 3% higher tenuring rate at unionized institutions in their sample, a reversal from only few years prior and in contrast to Brown and Stone's (1977a) finding of no significant difference. Gilmore's (1981) survey of more than 350 chief executives of unionized public 2- and 4-year institutions found that tenure and related personnel policies had increased across the board and had become more uniform, and Lee's (1979) study of six institutions found substantially increased faculty roles in personnel decisions because of unionization.

By the early 1980s, there was widespread agreement that collective bargaining formalized tenure and related procedures, potentially protecting probationary faculty from arbitrary decisions. Baldridge, Curtis, Ecker, and Riley (1978) further suggested that there could be a spillover effect where nonunionized institutions might adopt similar policies in an attempt to forestall bargaining. The literature in the years since has not suggested an alternate understanding (Wickens, 2008). Multiple studies pointed to the continued and increased inclusion of personnel policies in bargained contracts (e.g., Andes, 1982; Williams & Zirkel, 1988, 1989), including that tenure provisions are among the most profaculty provisions in contracts (Julius & Chandler, 1989). Wilson, Holley, and Martin (1983) found that 59.5% presidents of recently unionized campuses believed that unions had increased faculty job security, slightly but significantly less than the 62.5% who had believed such prior to unionization. McFerron, Camp, Lynch, and Woods (1996) found that statewide contracts often included many of the standards for tenure outlined in the 1940 Statement on Academic Freedom and Tenure, though none included all.

Tenure Rates, Gender, and Satisfaction

A subset of the literature has looked beyond formalized policies to consider issues such as promotion and tenure rates and satisfaction. Based on their survey at a single unionized institution, Elmuti and Kathawala (1991) found that more faculty were satisfied than not with the union's influence on promotion (40% satisfied, 23% not, and 37% with no opinion), tenure criteria (38%, 29%, and 37%), and termination-for-cause criteria (38%, 24%, and 38%). These rates of satisfaction were higher than for any other variable except representation of faculty interest to the legislature (42%, 20%, and 38%). In their national study, Lillydahl and Singell (1993) found that unionized faculty were more satisfied with job security, though not at a rate rising to a level of statistical significance. Based on two surveys at a single public institution, Ormsby and Orsmby (1988) similarly found increased satisfaction with promotion after unionization existed but was not statistically significant. Relying on the same data, Ormsby and Watts (1991) found female faculty members' satisfaction with promotion increased 25% after unionization, compared with 2.7% for males. Still, men were slightly more satisfied.

Benedict and Wilder (1999) considered unionization and rank attainment, finding a weak but significant relationship. Perhaps more important, they found that unionization might help reduce differences in rank attainment by gender, a finding that if more broadly true could explain Ormsby and Watts' (1991) findings. Using 1993 NSOPF data Perna (2001, 2003) found that working at a unionized institution was associated with higher probability of being tenured for both female and male faculty at 2-year colleges. It was less so but still significant at 4-year institutions. May, Moorhouse, and Bossard's (2010) examination of public research universities indicated that unionization was positively related to the proportion of women on the faculty and to women at the associate and full professor levels, holding other institutional factors constant.

Together, these studies revealed that unionization is consistently found to be associated with the existence of a tenure system and even more with the formalization of tenure procedures. Moreover, they suggested that being at a unionized institution might be related to the likelihood of being tenured and in a higher rank. Evidence further suggested that unionization might be associated with a reduced gender promotion gap, though even with unionization, disparities in tenure and promotion remain.

Retrenchment

Formalized tenure policies and procedural protections are important positive outcomes for faculty, but experiences in the 1970s demonstrated that the dismissal of tenured faculty during difficult economic times remained possible. Exact numbers are unknown, but thousands of faculty, many of whom were tenured, lost their positions for financial reasons (Rhoades, 1993). Amid these challenges, researchers began examining the effects of unionization on retrenchment policies, mostly through contract analysis, though occasionally through other means. Many of their findings pointed to the difficulties that faculty unions faced in preventing it; others pointed to the criteria used in determining who would be removed and on what justification. Only rarely, such as Johnson and Mortimer's (1977) study of the Pennsylvania state colleges, did the literature discuss union activity that forestalled retrenchment. In that case, union salary negotiations in early 1976 resulted in smaller raises than the union demanded but also in the rescinding of 82 faculty retrenchment orders. Brown's (1982) assertion that the University of Cincinnati's union contract provisions made it nearly impossible to remove faculty even during retrenchment is likewise an outlier.

Lozier's (1977) examination of 91 union contracts, almost two thirds of which covered faculty at 2-year institutions, found that 54 (59%) included a retrenchment clause, with no difference in their likelihood by either institutional type or bargaining agent. More recently negotiated contracts were more likely to have retrenchment clauses. The most common bargained justifications for retrenchment were financial conditions, program adjustment, and enrollment, with responsibility for determining if retrenchment was needed largely left to the governing board. The standard of financial exigency promoted by the AAUP appeared in only one community college contract but appeared in almost two thirds of 4-year institution contracts. Although some contracts offered exceptions for academic merit or program viability, seniority-related provisions including years in the position and tenure status were the most common criteria noted. Only three mentioned affirmative action. Nineteen of the 54 also specified that part-time faculty would be let go before full-time faculty. More than half of the contracts provided for faculty consultation on aspects of retrenchment, though most of the clauses were vague, and most provided some measures for reappointment.

Chandler and Julius's (1979) and Johnstone's (1981) later contract analysis showed even more attention to retrenchment but with similar overall patterns. Among the differences were greater faculty influence and more reliance on "financial exigency" in justifying retrenchment (Chandler & Julius, 1979). Echoing earlier studies, Lawler's (1982) examination of 22 contracts revealed that most did not mention who had the right to determine if exigency existed;

those that did largely assigned sole rights to the administration or governing board.

Kemerer and Baldridge (1980) and Baldridge et al. (1981) pointed to substantial differences in the percentage of formal retrenchment policies between unionized and nonunionized institutions. Only 37% of nonunionized institutions had them, whereas 77% of those unionized did, including 86% of unionized public college and universities. The data also revealed differences in the policies that did exist, with unionized institutions far more likely to provide for recall to positions (86% to 48%) and to include seniority rights (60% to 30%). The authors concluded that unionized institutions had greater procedural regularity and more avenues for appeal. And yet, the existence of bargained policies does not necessarily mean protection from retrenchment: more unionized institutions had experienced retrenchment than had nonunionized. That finding, though, might have said as much about the conditions of institutions at which faculty chose to unionize as it did about the influence of collective bargaining, as well as the reality of state budget problems. Regardless, the authors believed that the extent of retrenchment helped cool enthusiasm for collective bargaining in higher education.

Thousands more faculty were retrenched in the 1980s (Slaughter, 1993) and several scholars continued to examine contract provisions regarding it. Nasstrom (1986) discussed a no-layoff clause in the contract between the State University System of Minnesota and its faculty union, guaranteeing faculty with 20 years of experience or within 5 years of retirement stronger protections than tenure. Williams and Zirkel (1989) noted that retrenchment provisions were even more prevalent in 1985 (92.7% of contracts examined) than in 1975 (72.6%). Julius (1994) argued that retrenchment clauses in 2-year contracts were among the strongest assertion of faculty rights. Rhoades's (1993, 1998) extensive analyses of retrenchment policies provided some of the most important—and most recent—evidence, although much of it confirms earlier studies. His 1993 consideration of contracts from 42 institutions, systems, and districts with retrenchment clauses highlighted differences between 2- and 4-year institutions, as well as by bargaining agent, type, and control. Two-year institutions, for example, were far less likely than 4-year institutions to include AAUP language on financial exigency as a justification; public institutions were less likely than private. Contractual language in 2-year contracts emphasized different parts of the process than in 4-year contracts and offered different priorities about whom would be kept, with seniority more important at 4-year institutions. At the same time, across contracts, there was wide leeway in the potential justification for retrenchment, and administrators retained significant discretion in retrenchment decision. Faculty were largely provided meet and confer rights in the cases in which they had any rights at all.

Rhoades's (1998) examination of 178 contracts with retrenchment clauses revealed 42% lacked discussion of conditions that would be needed for laying off faculty. Most of those that did discuss them were at 4-year colleges and included economic rationales among other reasons; only a minority specified exigency. Again faculty often had no contractual rights to provide input, and administrators had ultimate authority in the overwhelming number of cases. Many contracts did, however, include rules regarding order, notice, recall, and reassignment which could complicate administrative efforts to reorganize the workforce, potentially making it unwieldy to remove tenured faculty, especially. This assertion did not go nearly as far as Brown's (1982) claim but did point to a role that union contracts can play in forestalling some retrenchment. Still, Rothgeb and Mitakides's (2015) survey of department chairs found no statistical evidence that unionized institutions were less likely to lay off faculty during financial difficulties.

In sum, Slaughter's (1993) contention about the relative ineffectiveness of unions in protecting against retrenchment captures a main thrust of the research. After noting that they were unable to negotiate "strong retrenchment clauses," she noted, "What protection unions did offer were usually centered on seniority. And even though contracts and personnel policies incorporated provisions that honored tenure and length of service, there was enough language providing for exceptions for discretionary managerial judgment as to render meaningless the faculty seniority provisions" (p. 262). Still, although they may not have been as strong as faculty advocates would have desired, the mere existence of clauses was more likely at unionized institutions and, for those they offered even limited protection, offered a benefit.

Overview of Research on Tenure, Grievance Procedures, and Retrenchment Policies

The research on personnel policies points to some union effectiveness in fostering tenure, promotion, and grievance procedures, especially formalized ones. This has been widely thought to reduce the arbitrariness of decisions, potentially explaining findings that unionization was associated with reduced gender rank and tenure gaps. There is less definitive evidence about whether unionization was related to tenure being easier to acquire overall. The analyses of retrenchment clauses and events highlight some gains but also shows that administrators maintain wide power to abrogate tenure and otherwise reorganize their faculties, even under union contracts. Moreover, the lack of consideration of affirmative action or related issues combined with the emphasis on seniority in many contracts highlight that whatever gains in equity have been made, they may ultimately remain tenuous.

Governance and Faculty Influence

The relationship of collective bargaining to shared governance and faculty influence has long been the subject of concern. Proponents have argued that unions can provide faculty input in institutional contexts where senates and other forms of faculty governance are powerless or, alternatively, can coexist with senates by focusing on issues outside of their purview. Critics have been less convinced, warning that unions encroach on traditional forms of governance, seek to expand their spheres of influence, and could even bargain away faculty roles for greater compensation. Moreover, as some faculty elect not to join the unions at their institutions, there has been concern over how and whether their interests will be represented on an organized campus (e.g., DeCew, 2003; Ladd & Lipset, 1973; Wickens, 2008; Wollett, 1974).

Early considerations of faculty unions warned of conflict between senates and unions, frequently pointing to difficulties at CUNY, where overlaps in jurisdictions occurred and led to significant disruption (e.g., Bain, 1976; Ladd & Lipset, 1973). McConnell (1971) cautioned that senates would become "relatively impotent" (p. 41) and Riesman (1973) pointed to presidents' beliefs that unions would eventually cause senates to atrophy. Begin (1974) highlighted the lack of actual research on the issue and addressed the concerns of bargaining critics based on his analysis of 26 colleges in New Jersey. He found multiple patterns of relationships between agents, senates, and administrations but little to fear, noting "there is no evidence to support a conclusion that collective bargaining has led to significant dismantling of the traditional institution-wide or system-wide governance procedures such as senates or faculty councils" (p. 584). Most unions and senates worked together, forming formal relationships that facilitated cooperation. As noted previously, Hedgepeth (1974) found that faculty authority in grievance procedures had shifted to the union, potentially undermining faculty control. Yet he equivocated on its overall meaning, as the faculty had previously been only advisory whereas the union could negotiate for formal roles. For many of his interview participants, the extent to which authority would shift remained an open question. Likewise, Garbarino (1975) argued that it was too early to tell what the effect of bargaining on senates would ultimately be but noted "unionization certainly has created more senates than it has eliminated, although it may have reduced the role of some senates in some types of decisions" (p. 144).

In multiple publications, Baldridge and Kemerer offered substantial early evidence on governance and collective bargaining, including that academic senates on unionized campuses were largely ineffectual prior to unionization and that they were rarely successful in becoming bargaining units (Baldridge & Kemerer, 1976; Kemerer & Baldridge, 1975). They found that bargaining units and senates largely operated in separate spheres but, based on Andes's (1974) contract analysis and the expressed fears of college and university presidents, warned that after initial contracts, unions would seem to expand the issues on which they bargained. Baldridge et al. (1981), Kemerer (1983), and Kemerer and Baldridge (1981), though, noted that their expectations of conflict had proven wrong and that senates and unions could together create a stable dual track of faculty influence. This finding, captured in the title to the latter work, "Senates and Unions: Unexpected Peaceful Coexistence," was supported by numerous other studies (e.g., Begin, 1979; Douglas, 1979; Lee, 1982; Mortimer & Richardson, 1977).

At the same time, several additional works pointed to the differential effects based on the influence of an existing senate. In her multisite case study, Lee (1979) found that institutions that had strong or long-standing senates maintained them but those with newly established governance structures saw them abolished or withered. As a whole, she argued, faculty "gained formal governance power through the union contract" (p. 581), even as administrative power became more centralized. Gershenfeld and Mortimer's (1979) consideration of bargaining in Pennsylvania's state colleges, which had young shared governance systems, pointed to increased overall faculty participation in governance but weakened senates. Gilmore's (1981) survey of college presidents also revealed that unionization had its greatest effect on institutions with weak governance structures.

Despite findings that faculty roles had increased, it was not always clear that they had gained additional power in governance issues (Cameron, 1985). Adler (1977) found that faculty believed that their power had increased through unionization but that administrators perceived it had not; some believed that administrative power had. The two groups likewise disagreed as to whether the influence of the senates had changed. Perhaps indicative of the larger state of understanding, the combined works by Baldridge, Kemerer, and associates highlighted that through unionization established senates had maintained and even expanded influence in academic matters, unions had increased power in economic areas, and campus administrators had increased power through new management tools and centralization, though the latter could be mitigated in multicampus systems as a result of increased system-wide centralization (e.g., Baldridge et al., 1981; Baldridge & Tierney, 1979; Kemerer, 1983; Kemerer & Baldridge, 1976; Kemerer & Baldridge, 1981). At the same time, Baldridge et al. (1981) pointed to the overall weak effect of unionization on faculty roles in governance—little had actually changed, although things had become more formal. These notions of formalization and centralization appeared in much of the literature both as specifically related to unionization and larger societal and economic pressures.

Richardson and Riccio (1980) surveyed administrators and faculty in 14 states, finding that both groups believed that faculty played larger roles in academic, administrative, and personnel decision making after unionization than they had before it. In a single state study, Decker, Hines, and Brickell (1985) likewise found that unionized faculty believed that they had more influence in 19 of 20 different areas of decision making than did nonunionized faculty; in 10 areas, the differences were statistically significant. Drummond and Reitsch (1995) echoed earlier studies noting the preexisting conditions of governance were influential in the power distribution after bargaining. Maitland and Rhoades (2001) reported that a 1998 survey of NEA leaders and members found little union influence in budgeting, merit pay and pay equity decisions, or the ratio of non-tenure-track to tenure-track faculty. Faculty were, however, very involved in academic, hiring, and tenure criteria decision making. Overall, the survey revealed that unionized faculty were more involved in governance, except in merit pay and faculty ratios. Still, they desired to be even more so.

Analyses of Contractual Governance Provisions

These surveys and related studies were joined by examinations of union contracts some of which showed an expansion of areas covered by contracts (e.g., Andes, 1982; Williams & Zirkel, 1988), although the implications were not always clear. Mere inclusion of an issue neither indicates to whom authority and rights are granted nor from whom influence might be withdrawn. To the extent that a senate or other faculty body previously had a significant governance role, union assertion of rights might shift influence from one faculty body to a more limited one. Where a minor role had existed, increased assertion of union authority might increase faculty influence. Based on his analysis of contracts, for example, Garcia (1975) argued that the very process of bargaining provided a governance role that would have been absent otherwise at community colleges.

Johnstone's (1981) examination of 89 bargained contracts at 4-year institutions revealed that only 37% explicitly discussed governance and even fewer (26%) included it as a stand-alone section or article. Among those that did, he found a range of approaches, including explicitly mentioning faculty rights in prescribed educational areas, incorporation of the AAUP's 1966 Statement on Governance of Colleges and Universities, the adoption of a preexisting faculty constitution, and procedural checks on university authority through requirements that certain decisions be made in consultation with—and at times, approval of—the faculty senate. Almost 20% included mentions of the faculty senate, with some considering them equal and others ascribing more power to either the agent or the senate. Johnstone noted the concern that unions could doom senates but found no evidence that they had. The overall picture was mixed with Johnstone concluding that his chapter on governance was not a "chronicle of a host of faculty and union success stories so far as their securing a more influential role in institutional governance" but was "full of examples of what might be gained," with "clear precedents for considerable democratization" (p. 131).

Almost two decades later, Rhoades (1998) similarly pointed to some union successes in protecting autonomy for individual faculty and in negotiating procedures that could delay administrator activities but argued that they needed to do much more to provide faculty input into strategic decision making, especially around the restructuring of the faculty workforce. Covering a range of areas, some of which have already been noted, he pointed to increased managerial discretion, including in areas such as instructional technology, through either explicit provisions or silence. He interpreted "the contracts to suggest that faculty are being professionally 'marginalized' (or are contributing to their own marginalization), bypassed by technological developments in the production process" (p. 205). In part, this was a result of changes at the "curricular periphery" (p. 206) where managers asserted control over the increasing part-time instructional force. The overall findings of the book were of increased reorganization for managerial flexibility and control, though faculty did retain authority in some areas. Community college faculty, for example, frequently maintained control of intellectual property and the autonomy to undertake outside employment through bargained contracts, though 4-year college faculty were less likely to do so. In a follow-up contract analysis, Klein (2010) asserted that institutions had inserted increasing amounts of control over intellectual property in the intervening years.

As part of their aforementioned article, Maitland and Rhoades (2001) found that more than one third of 294 contracts mentioned governance; almost a third mentioned senates. They concluded, as had others before them, that bargaining can reinforce shared governance where it exists and provides avenues for faculty input where it does not. At the same time, they urged faculty to pursue further contractual rights, especially in budgetary and strategic areas that touched on academic issues. Maitland, Rhoades, and Smith (2009) further pointed to governance, emphasizing that strong contractual language in areas of technology and distance education does exist in some contracts, though "most agreements impose relatively few limitations on administrations" (p. 82).

These works by Rhoades and others included consideration of community colleges contracts, but some focused explicitly on them, an especially important area considering the scope of bargaining and historic lack of strong shared governance in the sector. In her analysis of paired contracts from 1975 and 1985, Williams (1989) found that faculty achieved increased authority over employment decisions, teaching load, nonteaching responsibilities, and academic functions. Among 18 areas, only in grade alterations did administrative authority increase, according to contractual language. With only slight variations, these findings aligned with those in a similar study of both 2- and 4- year institutions that she had coauthored the previous year (Williams & Zirkel, 1988). Chandler and Julius (1985, 1987, 1988) and Julius (1994) presented findings from 15 years of studying locus of authority in community college contracts. They found that faculty authority remained relatively low as evidenced by contractual language but even limited authority was an improvement over the traditional lack of faculty voice in 2-year institutions. They also found significant differences by state and sector, with unionized faculty in private institutions attaining more authority than those in the public sector.

Kater and Levin's (2005) document analysis of 238 community college contracts considered faculty participation and management discretion in 16 areas, finding that the most frequently included areas of faculty participation were in grievance, curriculum, and faculty evaluation processes, although a minority of contracts did allow for input into areas such as budgeting and planning. The rights accorded to faculty in these and other areas were frequently for consultation or discussion, leaving ultimate decision-making authority up to the administration. And although some issues may have been left out of contracts because of institutional traditions that afforded faculty opportunities for influence, their absence provided further rights and discretion to management.

Renewed Interest in Governance

Lyne (2011), writing as the president of the United Faculty of Washington, argued that through unionization, shared governance was stronger than it had ever been on his campus, whereas the nonunionized state universities in his state had experienced setbacks in faculty roles. Bucklew, Houghton, and Ellison (2013) reviewed the existing literature on governance and unions, noting that bargaining agents could work in symbiotic relationships with senates or not. They offered four models of governance in contract language ranging from restrictive to comprehensive. More relevant, though, are two larger studies. Relying on 1993, 1999, and 2004 NSOPF data, Linville, Antony, and Hayden (2011a) found no difference in community college faculty members' perceived control of work by union status. On the other hand, based on a 2001 survey of presidents and faculty leaders at 903 colleges and universities, Porter (2013) found that both groups perceived that unionization had improved faculty influence in a number of areas, including salaries, appointments, curriculum, tenure, promotion, and teaching loads. On the specific issue of governance, both administrators and faculty viewed unions as having an influence, although only the former met statistical significance. He concluded that his "results indicate strong, positive differences between unionized and nonunionized institutions" in "faculty influence in decision-making" (p. 1205).

Overview of Research on Unionization and Governance

The research, then, does show some encroachment of faculty unions into areas that might have traditionally been covered by faculty senates or other forms of shared governance. "Might," though, is an important word, as most research suggested that this is most often the case at institutions at which faculty had historically low levels of influence in governance, such as community colleges, or that had recently lost it. Some senates have gone away explicitly because of unionization—either having been abolished or atrophied—but the weight of the evidence is that senates and unions can coexist and that in institutions without traditions of it, shared governance has improved. In many others, the union contract has served a protective function securing faculty influence either through the union or through existing governance means. At the same time that bargaining has increased, it has also formalized relationships and been linked to increasingly centralized power, especially in multicampus institutions. Of course, the broader changes in U.S. higher education in the late 20th and 21st centuries have had similar effects.

Collegiality and Campus Relationships

The finding that faculty unions and senates can, in Kemerer and Baldridge's (1981) terms, peacefully coexist points to another significant concern over unions on college campuses: how they affect campus relationships and collegiality. Certainly, faculty mistrust of the administration and dissatisfaction with relationships can be factors that contribute to organizing, and the bargaining process itself can be adversarial. Some argue that it is necessarily so, with Ladd and Lipset (1973) contending, "It is clear that the adversary relationship inherent in the very conception of collective bargaining does change the role and image of university administrators" (p. 88). Certainly, there is evidence that the bargaining process can be adversarial and fracture already divided campus relationships among and between various constituency groups, including faculty, administrators, and students. At the same time, there is also evidence that it is not necessarily the case that such will be the outcome and that in some situations the formality of the process and its outcomes can clarify roles and improve testy situations.

Some early case studies and firsthand accounts of bargaining pointed to worsening of relationships. Newton (1973) and Ladd and Lipset (1973), for example, noted a loss of collegiality at CUNY. Hedgepeth (1974) found that collective bargaining "extended and intensified" preexisting relational difficulties both within groups and between them at SUNY Cortland (p. 688). Seidman, Edge, and Kelley (1974) found that more than half of the faculty at the University of Hawaii believed that bargaining would bring increased conflict; Simson (1975) found that it did, with a fraught set of relationships among faculty, between faculty and administrators, and with union representatives. Yet the findings were not ubiquitous. Walters (1973) and Orze (1975), for example, pointed to the collegiality, trust, and a nonadversarial relationship in Massachusetts. Begin (1978) found that relations between faculty and administration had been maintained at Rutgers University, despite some discord at the bargaining table. Lee (1979) found extensive faculty and administration cooperation at three of her six sites and efforts to build trusting relationships at two more.

Other scholars examined issues related to collegiality, pointing to the formalization of academic relationships and concerns about the resulting changes (e.g., Gilmore, 1981; Kemerer & Baldridge, 1975). Especially prevalent in these are surveys of administrators expressing the belief that unionization would lead to increased conflict (e.g., Odewahn & Spritzer, 1976; Walker & Lawler, 1982; Wilson et al.,1983). Yet, the formalization of relationships does not inherently negatively affect those relationships. Over time, they might benefit from the contracted processes. Perhaps most thoroughly, Baldridge et al. (1978) highlighted these tensions, noting that more than 70% of presidents in their survey believed that bargaining resulted in more conflict, but only 42% of union chairs agreed. They not only noted the initial conflict with new bargaining agents but also pointed to the regularization of decision-making processes, the implementation of grievance procedures, and the maturation of bargaining relations as features that regulated conflict. Cameron's (1982) study of organizational effectiveness at 41 institutions found that both faculty and administrators perceived collegiality among faculty members to have decreased since unionization on their campuses, and collegiality among faculty and administrators to have decreased even more so. Yet Birnbaum and Inman's (1984) consideration of 18 pairs of institutions found that the differences in a measure of "shared purpose and morale among faculty and administrators" (p. 612) at unionized and nonunionized institutions were not significant. The authors suggested that this finding might counter expectations either because most commentary had come from administrators whose work had been disrupted or had focused on those most closely involved with actual bargaining. In either case, their perspectives might have been conditioned by expectations of adversarial bargaining rather than broader campus relations.

Moreover, Birnbaum (1984) found that the way in which bargaining took place could fundamentally affect relations; negative effects of contentious bargaining were replaced with increased trust and other positive outcomes when third-party mediators facilitated a productive negotiation process.

Direct examinations of the effect of bargaining on campus relationships have been quite rare in the past few decades. More frequently, issues of involving campus relationships and collegiality have been studied in terms of faculty satisfaction with multiple aspects of their jobs. In his examination of 4-year colleges in Pennsylvania, Hill (1982) found a weak but significant positive relationship between unionization and a measure of associational satisfaction, though one that included variables potentially related to both campus and off-campus relations. Finley (1991) found no significant differences in associational satisfaction at 10 paired 2-year colleges. Ormsby and Ormsby (1988) found no differences in satisfaction with coworkers before or after unionization at a single institution and, using the same data, Ormsby and Watts (1991) found no differences by gender, although it is unclear whom the faculty in the studies considered coworkers. At the same time, Ormsby and Ormsby (1988) noted that at the institution studied the union and administration were "starting to work jointly to correct problems that have created a hostile atmosphere" (p. 159). Lillydahl and Singell's (1993) consideration of data from more than 1,700 faculty at 4-year colleges found no significant differences in satisfaction with administration and faculty relations or quality of departmental leadership between unionized and nonunionized faculty, although they did find nonunionized faculty to be more satisfied with the spirit of cooperation among faculty and the quality of chief administrative officers.

Drummond and Reitsch (1995) argued that institutions with strong preexisting governance structures were more likely to remain collegial through bargaining, whereas those without them could see collegiality replaced by formality. Carlton (1995) and Dennison, Drummond, and Hobgood (1997) examined cases where bargaining was pursued collaboratively, pointing to the possibility of avoiding conflict-based bargaining. Castro (2000) sketched two case studies at community colleges, one where bargaining promoted a collegial work environment and one where it undermined it. Although pointing to the possibility of both positive and negative outcomes and suggesting that the approach to bargaining mattered in the collegiality outcomes, she offered few details. Arnold (2000) offered case studies of three state universities in New England, pointing to tension and acrimony amid organizing drives that could undermine long-standing cordial relationships.

Overview of Research on Collegiality and Campus Relationships

Although the work above offers some insight, it appears to be taken for granted that collective bargaining creates or exacerbates adversarial relationships, rather than closely examined. Certainly, testimonials and firsthand experiences pointed to strained campus relationships during organizing and bargaining. Some of the research has also suggested that unionized faculty are less satisfied with relationship after bargaining, and much has indicated that administrators believe that campus relations have been strained by bargaining. Yet the limited research evidence has also provided several counterexamples of bargaining relationships that have been successful through proactive presidential leadership, transparency, and trusting relationships. Also, as Birnbaum and Inman (1994) argued, much of the writing has emphasized the perspectives of those most likely to be negatively affected by bargaining, and little has considered change over time. The cross-sectional snapshots that predominate offer the potential to conflate causes of unionization with outcomes. The formalization of procedures that comes with contracts has often been cast in negative terms but at times has offered clarity and promoted conditions that can foster trust. As such, the potential for negative outcomes and reduced collegiality is clear. It is less clear, though, whether beyond the actual bargaining table, the long-term effects on collegiality are predominantly negative. In some cases, they can be positive.

Satisfaction

Issues of faculty satisfaction have been raised throughout this chapter and the previous one, so they are addressed only briefly here around global issues of job satisfaction or specific aspects of satisfaction not included elsewhere. The research points in multiple directions. In his study of 4-year colleges in

Pennsylvania, for example, Hill (1982) found unionization to be significantly associated with greater satisfaction in economic, teaching, administrative, and associational dimensions of work, arguing it provided evidence for greater overall satisfaction, though without a specific measure of it. Using similar measures at 2-year institutions, Finley (1991) found no significant positive associations with unionization and satisfaction, though negative ones relating to governance, support, and convenience. Neither Cameron (1982), looking at faculty and administrators, or Ormsby and Ormsby (1988) and Ormsby and Watts (1991), considering just faculty, found significant differences in overall satisfaction by union status. Neither did Gordon and Denisi (1995) in their consideration of three bargaining units in which union membership was not required.

Several studies considered factors related to satisfaction with the union (e.g., Castro, 2000; Elmuti & Kathawala, 1991; Van Sell, Barclay, Willoughby, & York, 2006) but much of the more recent research used NSOPF data to consider satisfaction more broadly. Lillydahl and Singell (1993) found nonunionized faculty to be more satisfied overall and in multiple areas of control over work, quality of environment, and support available, although unionized faculty were more satisfied with pay and benefits. Jacobs and Winslow (2004) included union status in their model of workload dissatisfaction using 1999 NSOPF data, finding no significant differences based on membership. Kim, Twombly, and Wolf-Wendel (2008) likewise included union status in their study of 2-year college faculty. Using 2004 NSOPF data, they determined that being a union member was negatively correlated with satisfaction with instructional autonomy for full-time faculty but not part-time faculty. Linville, Antony, and Hayden (2011b) considered 2-year college faculty with 1993, 1999, and 2004 NSOPF data. They determined that union status was not predictive of overall satisfaction and that in both union and nonunion environments, satisfaction with workload was the greatest predictor of overall satisfaction. In unionized institutions, control over work was second; in nonunionized institutions, satisfaction with benefits was second.

Myers (2011) argued that existing studies were limited by considering union membership as a dichotomous variable rather than one that allowed for choice and eligibility issues to be included. As such, she separated nonunionized faculty into those who were so by choice, because it was un-available, or because they themselves were ineligible. With 2004 NSOPF data for full- and part-time faculty at 4-year colleges, Myers used two-level hierar-chical linear models to account for both individual and institutional charac-teristics in her study of instructional and overall job satisfaction. In her most basic model of instructional satisfaction including only union status, faculty in all nonunionized categories had significantly higher satisfaction scores than unionized. In the full model, faculty who were not unionized by choice or un-availability reported significantly greater instructional satisfaction than union-ized faculty. In her most basic model of overall satisfaction, faculty who were not unionized by choice or ineligibility had significant higher satisfaction than unionized faculty. In the full model, only the former did. The nonunionized by choice faculty also reported significantly higher levels of satisfaction than the other nonunionized faculty. Myers acknowledged that the methods did not allow for a causal link but suggested that the results could be because of unionized faculty having unmet raised expectations or that the most impor-tant predictors were out of union control.

Concerned about endogeneity between job satisfaction and union mem-bership, Krieg et al. (2013) examined the effects of operating under a bar-gained contract regardless of actual union membership. Using all four cycles of NSOPF data in conjunction with data on when institutions initially bar-gained, they found working under a bargained contract to be significantly associated with wage and benefit satisfaction in the positive direction and workload satisfaction in the negative. There was no significant association for overall satisfaction. Importantly, when they examined union member-ship, rather than operating under a contract, they found union members to be less satisfied overall than nonunion members. Krieg et al. further considered the issue by position type, with tenure-line faculty following the same pat-tern as the overall group. For non-tenure-line faculty there were nonsignifi-cant positive relationships between unionization and overall satisfaction, as well as several other types. Only satisfaction with benefits was significant, though the authors caution methods and data might offer the explanation for such findings.

Overview of Research on Unionization and Satisfaction

These studies, along with those previously mentioned, demonstrate a complicated relationship between unionization and satisfaction. Unionized faculty
do not appear to be more satisfied overall than nonunionized faculty, and
multiple studies have found them to be less so. Union members appear to
be more satisfied with compensation although less satisfied with some other
aspects of their work lives, potentially indicating a trading that washes out
any overall effect. Importantly, dissatisfaction is associated with the desire to
unionize, raising directionality concerns for which the studies have difficulty
accounting. Although unionization might not itself reduce dissatisfaction, it
might not also be the cause. As Myers (2011) demonstrated, unionized faculty
appeared equally satisfied overall with those who were ineligible to unionize
or to whom it was unavailable. Plus, as Krieg et al. (2013) highlighted, even
if being in a union was associated with job dissatisfaction, operating under a
bargained contract was not.

Other Effects of Faculty Unionization

The main themes of the literature have been outlined but studies have looked
at additional issues in the decades since faculty bargaining began. Some of
these fall outside of the scope of this review, including those on legal issues,
differential effects by national affiliate, the dispersion of strike actions, and
bargaining strategies and roles. Others, though, are more relevant, including
a group that might be considered under the umbrella of university or organizational effectiveness. Cameron's (1982, 1985) aforementioned works are
perhaps the most prominent of these, examining nine areas of university performance and climate in an attempt to understand organization-level effects
based on faculty and administrator surveys. His 1982 study of 18 unionized and 23 nonunionized schools found that unionized institutions scored
lower on eight of nine dimensions of effectiveness (all but student career development). Only three differences, though, were statistically significant (student academic development, professional development and faculty quality,
and ability to acquire resources). At the same time, institutions with older
unions appeared to be more successful than those with more recent ones,

potentially pointing to increased ability to garner resources over time. Importantly, Cameron cautioned that his data were cross-sectional and many of his findings might be a result of the institutional characteristics associated with unionization, not the outcomes of unionization. Recognizing that his earlier findings had generated consternation, disagreement, and assumptions of causality, Cameron (1985) combined his initial 1976 survey with additional administrations in 1980 and 1983, though with reductions in numbers of institutions and responses. Using cross-lagged correlation to establish "temporal precedence" (p. 391) if not actual causality, he concluded that ineffectiveness led to unionization but that unionization did not decrease ineffectiveness over time. As nonunionized institutions became more effective over time, and unionized ones did not, the gap between them increased.

Birnbaum and Inman's (1984) study of campus climate included multiple organizational measures as assessed by two administrations of the Institutional Functioning Inventory at a set of matched institutions. Each of the 18 pairs consisted of one institution that was not unionized in either 1970 or 1980 and one institution that was not unionized in 1970 but was in 1980. In 1970, the institutions were significantly different in only one of 11 measures—academic freedom—with the institutions that did not then unionize scoring lower. In 1980, they were significantly different only in a measure of intellectual and aesthetic extracurriculum for students, a finding for which the authors had no explanation. There were, overall, almost no differences in measures of climate and effectiveness between unionized and nonunionized institutions either before or after collective bargaining. In light of other findings, the authors concluded, "recent research is building up a cumulative, consistent, and impressive picture of faculty collective bargaining as a process having surprisingly little impact upon important aspects of institutional life" (p. 615).

Much more recently, Cassell and Halaseh (2014) considered the relationship between collective bargaining and efficiency, measured in terms of core expenses per degree and per completion, and effectiveness, measured in terms of degrees and completions per 100 students. Controlling for school size, selectivity, and type, in addition to state-level variables, they found that unionized institutions were both more efficient and more effective. Cassell and Halaseh acknowledged that an explanation for the former could be that institutions that spent less were more likely to have faculty who unionize, but suggested that core expenses actually decreased the longer the institutions were unionized. Meador and Walters (1994) looked at very different measures of effectiveness—faculty and departmental research productivity—finding that unionization was correlated with lower research output and reputation.

Several studies have directly addressed the effect of unionization on organizational commitment, including Ormsby and Watts (1989), who found no significant changes in commitment to the university or academic unit based on unionization. Beauvais, Scholl, and Cooper (1991) examined commitment to the institution and union in the midst of and after difficult contract negotiations, finding that union membership did not lower organizational commitment and that organizational commitment increased after contract settlement. Likewise, Deckop, McClendon, and Harris-Pereles (1993) found little evidence that union membership was related to lower organizational commitment. Moreover, several studies have found that unionization is positively associated with retention (Nagowski, 2006; Rees, 1994) and negatively associated with intent to leave (Zhou & Volkwein, 2004) for certain groups of faculty.

Although these studies look at different issues and are too few and varied to be definitive, together they provide little evidence that unionization causes reduced institutional performance or negatively affects faculty members' commitments to their college or university.

Conclusion

College faculty collective bargaining received considerable attention throughout the 1970s and into the early 1980s, as researchers sought to understand the potential effects of a new phenomenon that threatened to upend higher education, either for good or ill. By the time the initial surge of union growth had subsided, a consensus was emerging that the effect was not as great as had been hoped by some and feared by others. Though reduced in number, the research studies in the decades since have largely confirmed this finding: unionization is associated with changes in faculty working conditions but those changes have been less drastic than might have been expected. There was early evidence for a faculty wage premium, though more recent evidence questions whether it exists or is significant, especially at 4-year institutions; whether there is a compensation premium is likewise unknown. Although individual situations vary, fears over the destruction of academic governance have been largely mitigated. The places that had strong governance have largely been protected and those with weak governance mechanisms have new routes to faculty influence. At the same time, managers retain significant discretion both within unionized institutions and across higher education. Perhaps the most robust example of faculty benefiting from unionization is in the formalization of tenure and grievance procedures, which may help offset some of the arbitrariness and opaqueness of vague and unspecified policies and procedures. This formalization, as well as the establishment of pay scales and the inclusion of some equity provisions in union contracts, is a potential explanation for some reduction in the gender-based differences, though as noted previously, significant disparities remain.

Among the biggest fears of unionization opponents was that bargaining would be divisive, impeding collegiality and undercutting organization commitment. Although those involved in actual bargaining have reported such, evidence indicates that bigger picture and longer term, the effects are not what had been dreaded. Moreover, although unionization might not be linked with improved satisfaction or organizational effectiveness, the negative correlations found seem to be more likely linked to institutional and systemic factors related to the causes of unionization as they are to the outcomes. Of course, considering the age of much of the research and both the contextual changes and methodological advances that have taken place, all of these conclusions could use further modern and rigorous evaluation.

Although more research is needed, the existing findings offer suggestions for practice and highlight that some arguments about collective bargaining for tenure-line faculty can be countered. Without clear evidence for significant compensation premiums, policy claims around escalating costs tied to unionization are problematic. Arguments that unions inhibit administrative flexibility are likewise undercut by contract analyses and evidence of substantial retrenchment even among unionized workforces—negotiated contracts often provide tenure-line faculty with more influence than they might have otherwise had but have not stemmed the push toward managerial discretion. Concerns over campus climate and collegiality may have more credibility, although adversarial relationships are not preordained and are more limited in scope than might be expected. Importantly, the approaches taken to organizing and bargaining and the expectations around them are crucial and can mitigate potentially negative outcomes. Over time, relationships can normalize and even improve. Despite benefits for faculty in governance, procedural protections, and related areas, collective bargaining has not been a panacea and has not caused radical change. Broader trends away from a largely tenure-line faculty have continued and wage gains have not been as great as advocates had hoped. As such, barring substantial changes in approach or outcomes, the expectations of both those who favor and oppose them should be adjusted accordingly. Of course, these issues must also be considered in light of local context and institutional situations. Even if, nationally, the evidence is suggestive of some union benefit for faculty with fewer negatives than feared, institutional policies and conditions are of fundamental importance and should drive both decisions about organizing and bargaining and the responses to them.

Non-Tenure-Line and Part-Time Faculty Unionization

U.S. COLLEGE CLASSES are largely instructed by faculty without the protections and security of tenure, and without the ability to earn them. The creation and widespread adoption of a tenure system in the middle of the 20th century has been followed by an erosion of tenure protections, increased hiring of part-time and full-time contract faculty, and a great stratification in the instructional workforce. Even within the large category of non-tenure-line faculty, there is tremendous variation, at times with concomitant variations in roles, responsibilities, and rewards. The group includes full-time lecturers on extended contracts, professionals from other fields teaching courses informed by practical experience, instructors trying to earn a living teaching part time at multiple institutions on a semester-by-semester basis, postdoctoral scholars in a liminal space, and many others who may or may not be seeking the stability and permanency that tenure provides. Together, non-tenure-line faculty make up two thirds of the instructional staff in U.S. higher education, whereas in 1969, they made up less than 25% (Schuster & Finkelstein, 2006). There are no indications that this trend will end soon, and although the extent of the reliance on non-tenure-line faculty differs by institutional type—2-year institutions rely on them more than 4-year institutions, and 4-year privates do more than 4-year publics (Dobbie & Robinson, 2008)—every sector of higher education is affected. Although many non-tenure-line faculty are credentialed and qualified similar to their tenure-line peers, and some bring skills and experiences that offer unique contributions, the conditions of their work can have negative consequences for student outcomes (e.g., Baldwin & Wawrzynski, 2011; Eagan & Jaeger, 2009; Ehrenberg & Zhang, 2005).

Not only are the numbers of non-tenure-line faculty growing, but their presence in unions is as well. The most recent evidence indicates that there are now more non-tenure-line faculty covered by bargained contracts than tenure-line faculty, and it has been the area of the most substantial union growth in the past two decades (Berry & Savarese, 2012). The research has not nearly kept up with that shift, as very few studies specifically examine any aspect of non-tenure-line unions, much less their effects. Following a brief discussion of the context of non-tenure-line faculty in unions, this chapter considers the research that has been done, including the early work on part-time faculty, the vast majority of whom operate off the tenure track. Because of the paucity of research, a somewhat broader body of literature is included than in the previous chapters. Together, these considerations pointed to concerns over the most appropriate bargaining units for non-tenure-line faculty and whether inclusions in broader units including tenure-line faculty is beneficial. They highlighted initial disappointment for those hoping for significant returns in the early years of bargaining, but substantial, if inconsistent, gains in the more recent past. As Adrianna Kezar, a leading scholar examining issues around the changing faculty workforce, recently argued, unionization "does empirically make a difference" (Flaherty, 2013, para. 3).

Background and Setting

Non-tenure-line faculty have necessarily been part in unionization in higher education from its beginning, as the creation of the modern tenure system arose decades after the AFT made its first inroads into higher education. Indeed, the standard tenure system was influenced by the AFT, which included senior faculty but was most attractive to the instructors and graduate students who felt ill served by their institutions during the Great Depression (Cain, 2012c). The beginning of widespread collective bargaining in the 1960s and 1970s brought with it new possibilities and potentially changing dynamics for faculty writ large and raised questions about the roles and place of non-tenure-line faculty in bargaining units. Based on organizing strategies and on competing NLRB rulings, non-tenure-line faculty have at times been included in bargaining units with tenure-line faculty and at times been excluded. The NLRB included part-time faculty in units with full-time faculty in its earliest decisions but in 1973 changed course and determined that they did not have a shared community of interest based on differing responsibilities and working conditions. Yet, later in the decade, the NLRB again allowed for combined units. State laws and rulings have varied as well, with some states allowing joint units and others establishing separate ones. These have worked both for and against non-tenure-line faculty seeking to unionize. So, for example, early units solely composed of non-tenure-line faculty were rare because of the tenuousness of their positions, so inclusion in broader units offered bargaining possibilities. Yet, in other cases, non-tenure-line faculty who sought to unionize were defeated when included in units with tenure-line faculty who did not. Whether non-tenure-line faculty are disadvantaged in the contracts negotiated by larger units has been an issue of some concern (Baldridge et al., 1981; Saltzman, 2000).

Although it was not always the case, organizing non-tenure-line faculty has become a priority for both the three large higher education unions and other labor organizations, most notably the SEIU. It has also been furthered by the existence of groups such as the New Faculty Majority and the Coalition of Contingent Academic Labor, activist organizations working to improve the conditions of the non-tenure-line instructors. Although much of the organizing has taken place at individual campuses, the past decade has seen significant effort to organizing non-tenure-line faculty—especially those on short-term and part-time contracts—on metropolitan bases. These efforts have started to bear fruit as non-tenure-line faculty in Washington, DC, garnered contracts at a set of doctoral universities, fostering similar efforts in cities across the country. And it is not just the educators who are in positions that are often termed adjunct who are unionizing; postdoctoral scholars, for example, have organized with significant success in the 21st century (Rhoades & Torres-Olave, 2015).

Research on Non-Tenure-Line and Part-Time Faculty in Unions

Shortly after widespread faculty bargaining began, Kemerer and Baldridge (1975) noted that part-time faculty at CUNY had not "fared well" (p. 81) as part of the larger bargaining unit, as unions had emphasized full-time faculty interests to the detriment of theirs. The authors remained optimistic, though, and suggested that bargaining might be most beneficial for faculty who were in the most tenuous positions, including assistant professors on the tenure track and non-tenure-line faculty. In their ASHE-ERIC report, Baldridge et al. (1981) pointed to that claim and reported, "Today, we are not so sure" (p. 25). The results of their 1979 survey revealed that the existing stratification had largely remained and "disenfranchised faculty gain less than expected" (p. 25). Dividing their sample by full and part time, they noted that most respondents indicated that the latter group had not experienced gains in pay, benefits, and conditions when working under bargained contracts. Although considerations of whether non-tenure-line faculty should be part of broader units, descriptive overviews of unit composition, and personal reflections on organizing continued to appear (e.g., Newcomer & Stephens, 1982; Swofford, 1984; Thompson, 1994), actual studies of effects were rare in the 20th century and have only recently become somewhat more abundant.

Contract Analyses

Beyond work by Baldridge and Kemerer, much of the early research on part-time faculty involved contract analyses, most often pointing to their entrenched subordinate positions relative to full-time faculty. An early consideration by Goodwin (1977) found that bargained contracts often worked to the detriment of part-time faculty by denying them eligibility for tenure, providing little input into governance, offering little in the way of benefits, and including clauses that made them the most vulnerable during retrenchment. Lozier (1977), too, found retrenchment clauses that benefited full-time faculty to the disservice of part-time faculty.

As part of a larger study, Leslie and Ikenberry (1979) undertook a more thorough content analysis of union contracts around part-time faculty issues, finding "many existing contracts are vehicles for the protection of full-time faculty" (p. 21). Contracts limited the number of part-time faculty, provided few or no job protections, and diluted due-process procedures. Although more than half included provisions for performance evaluation, few provided any recourse for part-time faculty during retrenchment. Still, Leslie and Ikenberry suggested that bargaining may have improved part-time faculty pay as 30% of the contracts they examined provided for prorated pay, compared with only 21% in a broader sample of both unionized and nonunionized institutions. In just over half of the contracts, part-time faculty were provided with some form of fringe benefits, though these were frequently contingent on a minimum workload. Interviews at three institutions with part-time faculty in larger bargaining units revealed intra-unit conflict, with full-time faculty often serving their own needs at the expense of part-time faculty. In sum, Leslie and Ikenberry concluded that part-time faculty had "not benefitted generally from the move to academic collective bargaining" (p. 25) and questioned whether unionizing either on their own or in combined units would prove useful for them.

Maitland (1987) analyzed 24 contracts covering part-time faculty in 22 community college districts and lecturers in the California State University and University of California systems. She found differences across contracts but concluded that bargaining had resulted in gains for "temporary faculty" in compensation, grievance procedures, and evaluations, though it had not provided equity with tenure-line faculty, who had started in a more advantaged position. She pointed to the conflict between temporary and permanent faculty in the same unit as the former are hoping to gain conditions that the latter had already secured. The latter also could be threatened by a strengthened and secured part-time labor force. Still, the fragmented nature of the part-time faculty led her to conclude that part-time faculty were better off in a broader unit than they would be on their own, even if unions could do more to improve seniority rights, security, and payment for work outside of classroom hours.

Rhoades (1996, 1998) pointed to the largely taxonomic and functionalist nature of the existing literature on part-time faculty that, although sensitive to part-time faculty needs, also accepted the need for managerial flexibility.

Taking an alternate approach, Rhoades used professionalization theory while exploring what bargained contracts covering 183 institutions revealed about managerial discretion and the conditions of part-time faculty work. The analysis revealed that 140 of the contracts made no mention of the conditions of appointment and release of part-time faculty; most of those that did dealt only with basic procedural issues of job posting and hiring. Only six contracts mentioned the release of part-time faculty, demonstrating the lack of procedural protections and the extent of managerial discretion. The contracts overwhelmingly included provisions regarding working conditions and layoffs that gave full-time faculty priority over part-time faculty and, where they existed, provisions regarding the collective workforce either provided administration discretion or limited the ratios and roles of part-time faculty. Almost half of the contracts that covered at least some part-time faculty did not address their rights or perquisites, a situation that Rhoades (1996) termed "striking" (p. 645) and a retreat from what Leslie and Ikenberry (1979) had found. Also in contrast to Leslie and Ikenberry, he found that few contracts provided for evaluation, and indeed, few specifically discussed duties. Taken together, these contractual provisions demonstrated substantial managerial discretion and the subordinate position of part-time faculty to full-time faculty, the latter of which Rhoades ascribed not just to full-time faculty protecting their own interests but to institutions doing the same.

In the 21st century, scholars have more directly addressed the broader group of non-tenure-line faculty. Based on analyses of contracts in combined and separate units in both 2- and 4-year colleges in California, Illinois, Michigan, and Oregon, Maitland and Rhoades (2005) argued "collective bargaining has improved the status and working conditions of contingent faculty" (p. 78) but presented a conflicted picture of non-tenure-line contracts. Gains in job security, seniority in hiring, and contract length had been achieved in some contracts, but were lacking in others. Across the board, administrations retained significant discretion in hiring, although, in contrast to Rhoades's (1996, 1998) earlier findings, most contracts addressed appointment, renewal, and nonrenewal, at times with provisions that benefited existing non-tenure-line faculty. Maitland and Rhoades (2005) pointed to a variety of compensation and benefit structures, but contract provisions often included pay by credit hour, tuition waivers, and professional development funds; some included health benefits and sick leave. They argued that the combined provisions showed a significantly better situation than that uncovered by Rhoades (1996, 1998) but argued that contracts still needed to be improved to protect and equitably treat non-tenure-line faculty. The following year, they expanded their considerations to all agreements in the NEA's Higher Education Contract Analysis System and again argued that faculty had experienced gains in areas such as job rights, evaluation, and compensation but that significant variations remained. They further pointed to the emergence of considerations of full-time non-tenure-line faculty and argued that unions needed to do more to include and bargain for them. More recently, Rhoades (2013) examined "just-in-time" hiring and "just-at-will nonrenewal" language in contracts for part-time faculty, again finding that some strong language to protect faculty rights existed, but it was far from the norm.

These contract analyses, then, demonstrated a shift toward greater protection for non-tenure-line faculty over time but with gaps and shortcomings relative to tenure-line colleagues. Rhoades's work, both alone and with Maitland, especially provided evidence of stronger language in a number of areas but also demonstrated that contracts are highly inconsistent; significant provisions exist but are far from ubiquitous.

Case Studies and Field Reports

These contract analyses have been supplemented by case studies and insider accounts of unionization among non-tenure-line faculty at multiple institutions. A number focus more on issues of organizing (e.g., Berry, 2005; Hoffman & Hess, 2009), but some include outcomes. Written largely by union proponents, members, and activists, most claim successes of bargaining. Zabel (2000) described the "extraordinary" results of bargaining at the University of Massachusetts at Boston, where, in 1998, part-time instructors teaching two classes a term (rather than the three a full-time faculty member would teach) were reclassified as "half-time employees with full medical, dental and retirement benefits, a floor of $4000 per course, a 16 percent salary increase over the three-year life of the contract, and an additional cumulative $200 raise every semester" (p. 15). In her reflective essay, Hoffman (2006) highlighted agreements on salary schedule, pay raises, and grievance procedures in California Faculty Association contracts with California State University.

Stubaus (2015) pointed to "significant gains" for non-tenure-line faculty at Rutgers University, the University of Illinois at Urbana-Champaign, and the University of Oregon, although in different ways. At Rutgers, the creation of a teaching non-tenure-line track and the possibility for promotion came almost 40 years after unionization. Unionization at Oregon is much more recent, with unit certification in 2012 and the first contract the following year. The agreement included the creation of a career track for non-tenure-line faculty, promotion eligibility, longer contracts, and mandated roles in unit governance. At Illinois, gains were made when the institution created a new category of "specialized faculty" in consultation with the university's senate and other groups at the same time that non-tenure-line faculty were organizing. Though providing greater protections than had existed before, the new union contended that the guidelines remained inadequate; it was certified as a bargaining agent in June 2014 (Stubaus, 2015). Nearly 2 years later, the union and university agreed to their first contract, which offered additional protections and multiyear contracts for faculty who were with the institution for 5 years or more (Wurth, 2016).

Cain, Budke, Wood, Sweeney, and Schwessinger (2014) described the efforts of their union, UAW Local 5810, for postdoctoral researchers at the University of California. They concluded that the union had provided immediate and important financial benefits, including a salary scale tied to federal standards and a 14% average pay raise. Camacho and Rhoads's (2015) study of the same case based on document analysis and semistructured interviews located postdoc unionization in the broader corporatization of U.S. higher education. They pointed to the vulnerability of postdoctoral workers, including through their frequent isolation in highly hierarchical laboratories and extreme dependence on the principal investigators (PIs) for whom they worked. Challenges to organizing included concerns about academic exceptionalism, administrative opposition, and difficulties in communication. Still, the final contract that was negotiated covered numerous issues that had been previously absent from postdoctoral policy at the university. Higher minimum wages, a more uniform salary scale, healthcare benefits, and a new grievance procedure with neutral third-party arbitration were all included. Camacho and Rhoads noted that the power dynamics between PIs and their postdoctoral workers remained challenging but "the organizers unanimously believed that the rights gained as a consequence of the bargaining process could not have been won and/or sustained without the union contract holding the UC administration accountable. Regardless of the degree to which their work environment changed after the ratification of the collective bargaining contract, there was a unified conviction that working conditions have improved" (p. 315).

Although these and similar treatments argue that unions have made gains for non-tenure-line faculty, considerations of the community and technical colleges in Washington pointed to a more complicated picture, especially in combined units. Smith (2003) acknowledged that multiple groups were involved but emphasized the Washington Federation of Teachers' role in achieving "three major victories" (p. 38) in the 1999 state budget appropriations: $10 million in funds for matching increases in part-time faculty salaries, expanded eligibility for retirement benefits, and the requirement that each college be requested to devise a strategy to both improve conditions for part-time faculty and decrease their use. Ruiz (2007) argued that these gains seemed significant in the moment but did little to change the overall inequities in the system. These inequities and the unions' emphases on the full-time members who dominated them led to substantial conflict between the unions and the Washington Part-Time Faculty Association (WPTFA), a "small band of rebel adjunct instructors" (p. 53). Through class action lawsuits, the WPTFA garnered health coverage and retirement benefits for faculty who work at least 50% time. In a broader piece, Hoeller (2009), a founder and leader of the WPTFA, further emphasized these divisions and the role of his organization, rather than the unions, in garnering additional raises and beneficial legislation for part-time faculty. Indeed, he pointed to successful 2006 efforts to get additional funds for part-time instructors and claimed that the union first opposed them to protect full-time faculty and then undercut their purposes. Fellow WPTFA leader Longmate (2010) likewise critiqued the unions in the state for negotiating for overload allowances for tenure-line faculty at the same time they sought to limit the number of courses non-tenure-line faculty could teach.

Beyond Cases and Contracts

A small but useful literature base has looked more broadly and systematically at these and related issues. As noted in the fourth chapter, Lillydahl and Singell (1993) used NSOPF data to consider multiple aspects of satisfaction at 4-year institutions. They found unionized non-tenure-line, as well as tenure-line, faculty to be significantly more satisfied with their total compensation, though not overall more satisfied. Dobbie and Robinson (2008) examined union density and contingency in the United States and Canada, although they cautioned that their study was based on "woefully incomplete" (p. 136) data. They found a lower reliance on non-tenure-line faculty in cases where non-tenure-line faculty had been organized for longer periods of time and had the power to diminish compensation and security differences between tenure-line and non-tenure-line faculty. In situations where union density was low and the unions had not reduced the differences, unions had no effect on the use of non-tenure-line faculty. Where tenure-line and full-time non-tenure-line faculty were organized and powerful, but part-time faculty were not, union density increased the use of non-tenure-line part-time faculty.

Cross and Goldenberg's (2009) analysis of non-tenure-line faculty at 10 research universities revealed improving practices around security and benefits, as well as access to grievance procedures at all institutions, regardless of unionization. They emphasized beneficial practices at nonunionized institutions and suggested that uniformity in contract language across campuses could have negative effects. Their study did not, however, consider whether any of the practices were in response to threats of unionization, whether the unionized faculty became so because their institutions were not providing them with conditions available elsewhere, or other potential causes and effects that might not be apparent in a narrow window. Moreover, at least one of the institutions is currently in the midst of a significant organizing effort among its non-tenure-line faculty.

In 2012, the Coalition on the Academic Workforce (CAW)—a group of 26 higher education associations, unions, disciplinary associations, and related organizations collaborating to study and improve the working conditions of non-tenure-line faculty—released the results of a survey of more than 10,000 part-time non-tenure-line faculty. Although this was not a representative sample and the survey relied on descriptive statistics without, for example, controls for cost of living or other factors, the report pointed to differences in compensation and conditions of unionized versus nonunionized part-time faculty. Median course salary was $3,100 at unionized institutions and $2,475 at nonunionized institutions; a union wage premium existed for all institutional types except baccalaureate colleges. More than 34% of unionized faculty reported health benefits from their institution, compared with less than 14% for nonunionized. Over 60% of unionized employees had retirement benefits through their institution, compared with 27.5% of nonunionized. Faculty who were on campuses with a union similarly reported higher levels of pay for class cancellations (17.9% to 9.9%), payment for departmental meeting attendance (9.7% to 5.4%), payment for office hours (14.5% to 3.8%), regular salary increases (33.9% to 12.1%), job security (19.4% to 3.9%), tuition assistance (21.8% to 15%), and professional travel funding (18.3% to 10.7%), among other types of institutional support. Only in very few cases was the reverse true and the differences were very narrow (e.g., 77.5% of unionized faculty had library privileges and 79.2% of nonunionized faculty had them).

As part of their study of academic deans' attitudes toward and policies regarding non-tenure-line faculty, Gehrke and Kezar (2015) considered the effects of unionization on both full- and part-time faculty. Based on survey responses of 264 deans, they concluded "the benefits of unionization are evident throughout these [statistical] analyses, particularly for part-time faculty" (p. 948). Unionized part-time faculty were more likely to have medical benefits and family leave than their nonunionized peers. Both part- and full-time faculty on unionized campuses were more likely to receive multiyear contracts than those not on unionized campuses, and unionization was negatively associated with committee work for full-time faculty. All of these findings were statistically significant. At the same time, a small portion of the respondents to open-ended questions indicated that the contracts constrained their ability to create policies to increase participation in governance and related activities.

Kezar's (2013) qualitative study of non-tenure-track faculty members' perceptions and experience of support at three master's institutions focused elsewhere but found that "unions shape beliefs or feelings of support" (p. 11).

As one participant in her study noted, "knowing the union is there and is negotiating to get us professional development days and paid office hours makes me know that things are getting better, that I will be better able to do my job" (p. 24). At the same time, the union effect was more about general campus environment than any department-level issue, and some longtime non-tenure-line faculty remained distrustful of unions.

Conclusion

In sum, despite some useful recent work and older contract analyses, the research evidence on the effects of unionization is thin. Still, it highlights benefits for non-tenure-line faculty in terms of pay, job security, contract length, benefits, and institutional support. The recent research demonstrates few negatives for organized non-tenure-line faculty, with the exceptions of contracts potentially limiting administrators' abilities to further include them in governance and the prioritization of full-time members in some units. That said, both older research and firsthand accounts point to the potential for conflict in joint units, where interests of faculty with different statuses can be pitted against each other. Also, some literature suggests that unions could do even more and calls on them to adopt the language in existing contracts that offers the strongest protection for non-tenure-line faculty.

The limited literature on these unions, as well as the great diversity in the makeup of the non-tenure-line faculty, leaves numerous opening for scholars to address. The largely insider accounts of organizing and bargaining should be supplemented with additional rigorous scholarship on individual and multiple cases to point to the further complexity of the issues. More work that gathers and examines national data on effects on salaries, job security, governance, satisfaction, and working conditions is needed, especially that which considers context and controls. The full range of non-tenure-line positions and the potential differences in experiences should be considered as well. With continuing concerns about bargaining unit makeup and whether broad units will best serve the least advantaged within them (e.g., Greenberg, 2014; Hoeller, 2010), different outcomes related to unit makeup require much more examination. Finally, news reports and historical analyses have argued that efforts to organize unions without bargaining rights can still garner positive results for their members (e.g., Flaherty, 2014), suggesting further avenues for research in the modern era.

Although this additional research is needed to consider the full range of effects, including on the institutions at which unionized non-tenure-line faculty serve, the evidence provides clear support that collective bargaining has benefits for part-time and non-tenure-line faculty and justifies the increased efforts to organize them. It also points to some exemplar policies and contract clauses that can serve as models for future bargaining efforts. Though some of the evidence dates to before the modern recognition of higher education's staffing crisis, it highlights that non-tenure-line faculty may be best served by stand-alone units. It likewise points to the need for broader bargaining units to meet the needs of their diverse membership, a particularly important concern in light of the shifting makeup of the faculty workforce. To the extent that these findings remain after further study, the improved conditions and stability that can be bargained for offer substantial benefits. Importantly, if research suggesting that the conditions of faculty work are linked to student outcomes is accurate, these benefits might extend beyond the individual faculty members to the students whom they educate.

Graduate Student Unionization

E VEN MORE THAN faculty bargaining, collective bargaining by graduate students has been highly contested in U.S. higher education and remains so today. Largely localized in research universities, including in some of the most elite institutions in the nation, graduate student unions argue that their members' teaching—and at times administrative and research—roles no longer serve as forms of apprenticeship but are instead poorly compensated labor. Moreover, with a bleak academic job market, many graduate student instructors question the purpose of such an apprenticeship. For more than two decades, graduate students have been a central focus of organizing efforts in higher education, attracting new national affiliates and raising fundamental questions about roles and structures in U.S. higher education. Despite some very good work, the research has not kept up with the growth in the number of graduate students covered by collectively bargained contracts—some 64,000 according to Berry and Savarese (2012). This chapter reviews the research that does exist, supplementing it with additional firsthand and historical accounts. In so doing, it highlights studies that have sought to understand reasons for graduate student decision making and the outcomes of collective bargaining, including findings that cast doubt on claims that unionization is harmful to student–faculty relationships.

Background and Setting

The roots of graduate student unions are in the Depression-era AFT campus locals, many of which were populated by graduate students and temporary instructors, at times to the chagrin of AFT leaders who desired more established and prestigious faculty (Cain, 2012c). Student protests in the 1960s and the larger shift toward labor in higher education brought with them a push for bargaining among graduate students culminating with the successful efforts at the University of California-Berkeley, the University of Wisconsin, the University of Michigan, and a handful of other institutions—including Rutgers University, which has both faculty and graduate students in the same bargaining unit. The real momentum for graduate student unions occurred around the turn of the century, with students at dozens of institutions seeking bargaining rights and affiliations with national organizations (DeCew, 2003; Schneider, 1997). Battles at institutions such as Yale University and New York University were hard fought, raising legal challenges and charges of retribution and unfair labor practices. Efforts to unionize at the former were unsuccessful, though labor organizers claimed credit for the university's decision to raise students' stipends—a claim that the university denied (DeCew, 2003). Following a 2000 NLRB ruling in their favor, a UAW-affiliated union at NYU successfully bargained a contract in 2002. It was a short-lived success as the NLRB reversed course in a 2004 case involving Brown University and NYU withdrew recognition of the union when the first contract expired. Efforts at Brown, Tufts University, and other private institutions were likewise stifled and graduate student unionization remained a public university phenomenon—all 64,424 members of graduate student unions in the 2012 directory were at public universities, many of them among the most renowned public institutions in the country.

In 2013, following years of union activism and organizing, NYU acceded to union demands and again agreed to bargain. By the time that the two sides agreed to a contract in early 2015, the Graduate Workers of Columbia had affiliated with the UAW and filed for their own certification as a bargaining agent under the NLRB. On August 23, 2016, the NLRB overturned the Brown decision and ruled that the graduate students had employee relationships with their universities. They were therefore eligible to collectively bargain, potentially launching a new era of graduate student unionization (Patel, 2016). The reaction was swift and highlighted the contested nature of graduate student organizing. Yale University president Peter

Salovey expressed concern that student–faculty relationships "would become less productive and rewarding under a formal collective bargaining regime" (Flaherty, 2016a, para. 13). Lawyer Joseph W. Ambash (2016), who had argued the earlier Brown case and written an amicus brief on behalf of a number of elite universities, claimed that it would "have a profound and unfortunate effect on private higher education as we know it." Molly Corbett Broad (2016), president of the American Council on Education, added that it was guaranteed to increase the cost of college, was an example of federal regulatory overreach, and would fail a court challenge. Yet, many others celebrated decision, with the AAUP's Howard Bunsis claiming it was a "tremendous victory" (Flaherty, 2016a) and AFT president Randi Weingarten (2016) calling it "a great day for workers." *The New York Times* lauded the decision and editorialized that graduate student assistants "are essentially low-paid, white-collar workers, ... most of whom will never get tenure-track positions" (Editorial Board, 2016, para. 7). And organizers at private universities across the nation ramped up efforts that had begun in anticipation of the ruling.

The divergence in published reaction was profound—and the responses in the comment sections of leading trade and news publications were even more so. It was also indicative of the long-standing disagreements over the benefits and costs of graduate student unionization and whether graduate student assistants are employees when teaching and working in labs. DeCew (2003) noted that many administrators and faculty members view the issue through a guild model, where graduate assistants are apprentices and unions would interfere with personal relationship and training; a corporate model of higher education upends this view. In support of unionization, she pointed to the historic success of unions at the Universities of Wisconsin and Michigan, the changes in the faculty job market that problematized the apprenticeship model, increased teaching loads that hinder academic progress, increasingly distant faculty–student relationships, financial gains for student workers at both unionized institutions and those seeking to forestall organization, psychological benefits that accrue to students who feel empowered, and the potential to bargain for improved teaching conditions. Opponents counter that academic and economic issues cannot be separated, unionization can inhibit academic freedom and judgment, unionization can further divide faculty and students, national affiliates are taking advantage of students, and other routes for improving working conditions and experiences exist. Yet despite the fact that graduate student unions remain a key and disputed issue in U.S. higher education, little research has been undertaken on them; almost none explicitly considers outcomes beyond a single case.

Research on Graduate Student Unions

Much of the writing on graduate student unionization weighs in on questions of whether graduate students are employees, arguing for or against the proposition or highlight differing perspectives on the issue (e.g., Hayden, 2001; Rhoades, 1999). Other studies pick up on these debates and offer overviews of unionization, pointing to the historical development and current scope of bargaining, and suggesting possibilities for future research (e.g., DeCew, 2003; Singh, Zinni, & MacLennan, 2006). These are joined by studies that emphasize the legal debates and rulings that have set the context for and determined the scope of bargaining efforts, while also revealing their contested domain (e.g., Saltzman, 2000). Each of these is important and raises issues addressed in the opening chapters but more relevant here are the firsthand and historical accounts of organizing; the studies of causes, correlates, and ideologies of those who organized; and most significantly the outcomes of bargaining by graduate student employees. Each is discussed in the following sections.

Firsthand and Historical Accounts
One strand of the published writing on graduate student unions is in the form of first-person accounts of organizing efforts, strikes, and negotiations. In the aftermath of the Teaching Assistants Association's (TAA) first contract at the University of Wisconsin, for example, participants reflected on the issues involved and processes undertaken. Sherman and Loeffler (1971), advisor and counsel to the union, respectively, framed the decision to unionize in terms of the changing university, the pursuit of research excellence, the devaluation of teaching, and the poor job market for PhD recipients. They noted that

pay, working conditions, and burdensome time demands were all influential. Feinsinger and Roe (1971), who served as mediators in the dispute, emphasized the process of negotiation and the competing proposals offered by the two sides. They noted that the most challenging issue was the union's demand that it have shared responsibility for educational policy at the departmental level. It was a demand that was ultimately unmet. Feinsinger and Roe also pointed to the legislature's threat to cut out-of-state tuition waivers in half as a precipitating factor. Christenson (1971), a member of the university's negotiating team, emphasized the need for legislation to define the legality and scope of bargaining and the challenges posed by dual student–employee status. TAA president Steven Zorn's (1971) early analysis noted that the union strike ended in a stalemate, was unable to shut down the institution, and did not garner all that the union wanted. It did, though, provoke enough trouble to cause some concessions. At the same time, the strike evinced an attitudinal shift among union members, increasing their militancy and willingness to challenge the faculty. Decades later, Czitrom (1997) reflected on his years as a shop steward in the early 1970s, emphasizing the union's "radical critique of the university" (p. 218) and efforts to link with the larger labor movement. A handful of works by those not intimately involved have covered these same themes (e.g., Van Ells, 1999). Most comprehensively, Craig (1986) examined the entire history of the local, which had its bargaining ability withdrawn by the university in 1980. She argued that its continuing emphasis on educational policy influence and threats of strike ultimately led to its demise.

Other early graduate student unions have received less treatment, although Ingerman (1965) pointed to the roots of AFT Local 1570 at the University of California, Berkeley, in that institution's Free Speech Movement and highlighted the difficulties in negotiating on a campus-wide basis. Dubin and Biesse (1967) further detailed the union's founding as both a local outgrowth of student protest and part of larger shifts in higher education staffing and concerns over the place of graduate students in the profession. Though focused more broadly, Aussieker (1975b) pointed to its decline in the early 1970s while also noting other student attempts to engage in bargaining.

The emergence of a broader movement at the end of the century brought a number of published works about organizing by union members and their supporters. The Graduate Employee and Student Organization at Yale University, for example, was the subject of two issues of *Social Text*, the first of which included the proceedings of a strike symposium and became the basis for the edited volume *Will Teach for Food* (Nelson, 1997). The combined pieces include larger critiques of the changing nature of higher education and its exploitation of workers, as well as details of grievances and difficulties at Yale. So, too, do other insider accounts (e.g., Johnson & McCarthy, 2000). The ultimately successful organizing and bargaining efforts at the University of Iowa have likewise been treated in numerous pieces that point to both the underlying economic reasons and the importance of social justice issues for unionizing (e.g., Barba, 1994a; Schmid, 2001; Scott, 2000). The edited volume *Cogs in the Academic Faculty* (Herman & Schmid, 2003) is grounded in the Iowa experience and includes history and analyses of the Iowa drive and negotiation, which were influenced by the local's identification with organized labor, inclusion of social justice issues, and commitment to rank-and-file democratic practices (Breitzer, 2003). It also considers of graduate student unionization at the University of California, Santa Barbara (Sullivan, 2003) and the University of Florida (Thompson, 2003) in addition to larger issues of organized academic labor. Krause et al. (2008) offer perhaps the most in-depth treatment of graduate student organizing at a single institution, detailing the 2005–2006 Graduate Student Organizing Committee/UAW strike at NYU as seen through a frame of the corporatization of higher education.

These and additional insider treatments from across the nation (e.g., Gross, 2006; Johnson & Entin, 2000) offer insight into the reasons for unionization, the experience of graduate student organizers, the belief systems that have propelled them to organize, and the challenges that are posed. Together, they point to driving issues that include compensation, fundamental workplace rights, grievance procedures, social issues, and broader shifts in higher education that particularly affect low-paid graduate instructors both in the moment and in their potential careers.

Causes, Correlates, and Ideologies
Scholarly attention to issues of graduate student unionization increased in the early 21st century, with many studies emphasizing issues related to causes and

ideology more than effects. Embedded within DeCew's (2003) larger consideration of the arguments about and efforts to organize graduate students was a "brief survey" (p. 97) of organizing efforts in the opening years of the century. It revealed an emphasis on traditional bread-and-butter issues including wages, stipends, healthcare, and, in some cases, childcare. Unions were likewise concerned with ameliorating disparities in wages across departments and, to a lesser extent, workloads and job security.

Rhoades and Rhoads (2003) undertook a discourse analysis of the public presentation of graduate student unions based on a purposeful sample of 10 union websites. They found that multiple identities could and did exist, but building a collective identity "around a sense of being a 'marginalized worker'" (p. 175) was key to the unions' public presentations. Additionally, traditional union issues of wages, healthcare, benefits, and protections were the most prominent ideological positions, but each of the sites also addressed professional issues about quality of instruction and projected the professional identities of their members. At the same time, participatory democracy was highlighted, often in contrast to ascribed university positions and functioning, as was a commitment to diversity. Finally, the unions' websites connected the local efforts to those of graduate students elsewhere, though largely not to broader undergraduate student movements; spoke directly to faculty but not their organizations; linked to international graduate student unions but showed little evidence of having learned from their experiences; and displayed wide variation in sophistication. Rhoades and Rhoads argued that these public discourses revealed graduate student unionists as connected with national organized labor but not local workers and looking toward professional professorial roles without fully considering the labor concerns that they will face in those roles.

Rhoads and Rhoades (2005) later examined graduate student unionists' "critique of 'corporate academy'" (p. 245), being clear that it was not the driver of unionization—wages, healthcare, working conditions, and related issues maintained primacy. At the same time, their multisite case study involving unionization at four institutions demonstrated significant and widespread concern about perceived corporate practices in higher education, including corporate partnerships, a perceived emphasis on economic factors over student and employee well-being, and, to some, a connection to globalization. Study participants indicated concern about a management culture and the exploitation of graduate student and temporary instructional labor.

Rather than focusing on the views and ideologies of organized students, Lee et al. (2004) undertook a qualitative case study of organizing efforts at UCLA to understand the "cultural barriers" to unionizing. They found that student transience and time demands, the conflicting roles of students as employees, and the preparation for and alignment with a professional role—which some saw as in opposition to unionization—impeded student organizing activity. The loose coupling and autonomy of faculty work, which the authors linked to the cosmopolitan nature of a research university, and the paternalism of administrators also presented obstacles. Importantly, strained relationships with faculty did not present a barrier, despite concerns in the literature to the contrary.

Several more studies have looked for correlates of support for unionization among graduate students. Based on two surveys of graduate students immediately after union elections, Blader (2007) found that beliefs about the existence of procedural justice and the potential of a union to improve it were significant predictors of support for unionization and voting behavior. Identification with the organizing unit was likewise a significant predictor, one that could partially mediate procedural justice and union instrumentality beliefs. In the aftermath of several elections that rejected bargaining, Chanvisanurek, Rubin, Kearns, Rubin, and McCoy (2007) surveyed members of the Graduate and Professional Student Organization at Indiana University. Through regression analysis, they found that broader views on organized labor were the most significant predictors of propensity to unionize, followed by working conditions, union influence, and job satisfaction. Neither inequity perceptions nor wages were statistically significant. In a similar study at the University of Illinois, Rubin and Rubin (2007) found perceptions of organized labor and working conditions to be predictive. Both studies are suggestive of the need to look broadly for determinants of unionization.

Some of the best evidence comes from Julius and Gumport's (2002) comprehensive article providing an overview of graduate student unionization and an analysis of both its causes and outcomes, the latter of which are addressed in ensuing pages. Based on interviews on 20 campuses and analyses of archival data and union contracts, they argued that the catalysts for unionization included the increased time to degree and the concomitant economic difficulties. They pointed to the changing nature of faculty roles and the devaluation of teaching, arguing that teaching assistants were performing roles faculty would have in earlier era but they were roles that were now less respected. State legislative context, campus politics, and local faculty unionization were important as well. Although unionized faculty were more supportive of the unionization of graduate students than those who were not, there remained important differences between organized faculty and graduate students, the latter of whom were more likely to be at prestigious institutions, to emphasize salaries and working conditions, and to be represented by unions other than the three main educational unions.

Effects

If the relative lack of research-based literature on graduate student unionization overall is noteworthy, the paucity of studies of its effects is even more so. The aforementioned accounts of TAA emphasized organizing and negotiation issues but mentioned contracted outcomes, including the improvements in wages and guarantees around working conditions such as class size. Craig (1986) pointed to the ongoing efforts of the union to exercise greater power over teaching and curricular functions as causing difficulties with the faculty. Barba (1994b) examined five graduate student contracts, finding formalization of hiring and grievance procedures, sick and parental leave benefits, and, usually, salary scales. Schmid (2001) pointed to a minimum of 15% raises under the union contract at Iowa, with some graduate assistants' wages increasing 30% but little other research has been undertaken. Indeed, Hewitt (2000) wrote that his literature review unearthed "no empirical studies conducted on the topic of graduate student collective bargaining" (p. 157).

Faculty–Student Relations. Perhaps the central concern involving graduate student unionization relates to its potential effect on relationships between students and their faculty mentors. Preserving those relationships, as well as the underlying apprentice model of graduate training, is among the most prominent arguments put forth in opposition to student bargaining

(DeCew, 2003) and has been a key issue in NLRB rulings on the topic. To date, the research has not demonstrated that substantial concern is warranted. Hewitt (2000) examined faculty attitudes and beliefs through a survey of liberal arts and sciences faculty at five universities with graduate student unions. He found substantial support for unionization broadly and in higher education specifically, as well as a strong belief that graduate assistants should be considered employees with the right to bargain to protect themselves from mistreatment. More than 90% of the respondents indicated that student bargaining did not interfere with their ability to teach or advise graduate students, and 87.9% indicated that it did not inhibit mentoring relationships. The open-ended responses to the survey were largely positive about unionization but indicated a range of prounion, antiunion, and neutral views. Faculty across the spectrum expressed concern for the time students spent on union activities, the financial implications of negotiated contracts especially in the natural sciences, and the procedural burdens a union could place on them.

Julius and Gumport (2002) investigated these issues more fully and found occasional concern that there could be negative effects on faculty–student relationships but no actual evidence of them. Indeed, a number of their interview participants indicated that bargained contracts could improve relationships by setting clear boundaries and lines of communication. Their examination of contracts and arbitration decisions also found no evidence that bargaining negatively affected mentoring relationships. They suggested that a partial explanation may be that students view the larger university as their employer, not the faculty with whom they work. Although acknowledging that some relationships could get difficult—especially for senior administrators, those with little labor relations experience, and in cases where lengthy battles over the right to unionize has increased militancy—and that the potential exists for challenges arising out of grievance processes, there was no basis to argue that it actually has happened. Moreover, "the professional orientation of faculty as mentors and teachers is apparently not jeopardized by unionization" (p. 206).

Two studies considered the issue from students' perspectives. Lee et al.'s (2004) aforementioned case study emphasized other issues but noted "graduate students did not feel that unionization negatively affected their relationships with the professors" (p. 355). More directly, Rogers et al. (2013)

examined student views on faculty relations and academic freedom in the first study to compare experiences of unionized and nonunionized graduate students. Based on 516 usable survey responses from graduate students employees at eight institutions (four matched pairs of unionized and nonunionized institutions), they concluded that unionization either has no impact or a positive impact on faculty–student mentoring relations, as well as many other outcomes. They suggested that this could be because unionization "encourages management to rationalize practices, encourages stronger mentoring practices," (p. 507) or shifts the employee relationship from student–faculty to student–administration. They also found weak support for a positive impact on the climate for academic freedom.

Salaries. Even less research has explicitly examined issues related to effects on salaries. Ehrenberg, Klaff, Kezsbom, and Nagowski (2004) relied on an anonymized data exchange of 29 major universities from 1996–1997 through 2000–2001. The institutions were divided into four categories— those that were not unionized, those that were unionized before 1995, those unionized by the end of 1996, and those unionized beginning in 1999– 2001—and analyzed in terms of average stipend, average academic year compensation (excepting healthcare), average academic year cost to the institution, average summer salary, and average salary of TA as a proportion of the average salary of assistant professors (as a measure of cost of living). The different analyses yielded slightly different results, though the groups to unionize in the last period largely received the highest salary and compensation but were also in areas with the highest cost of living. They concluded, "The findings suggest that the impact of graduate assistant unions on economic outcomes does not appear to be very large and that concern over graduate student unions may be overstated" (p. 230).

Schenk (2010) used data published in the *Chronicle of Higher Education* from 2000–2001, 2001–2002, and 2003–2004 to examine salaries, compensation, and wage differentials at a sample of institutions that had bargained contracts, unions but no contracts, and no unions. He found that graduate students at institutions with union contracts had statistically significant higher salaries but not higher total compensation, suggesting that wage gains might be otherwise offset. He found no differences in the likelihood of health benefits, department-based wage differentials, or salaries for research assistants between unionized and nonunionized students. Rogers et al. (2013) found statistically significant positive impact on perceptions of both pay equity and pay adequacy. In the full national model, unionization was positively correlated with salary but only weakly ($p > .10$). They concluded there was "some support for the notion that unionization improves the economic terms of graduate student employment in the form of annual stipends" (p. 507). At the same time, concerns about potential difference between nominal and real salaries, stipends and total compensation, and the contentions that some institutions raise stipends either to compete with unionized institutions or to forestall unionization leave questions unanswered.

Conclusion

The New York Times (Editorial Board, 2016) editorial lauding the NLRB ruling in the Columbia University case concluded, "The question going forward is the extent to which those new unions will help improve working conditions in academic life" (para. 8). The existing empirical literature offers little clear guidance. The best evidence is that it will do no harm to graduate student compensation and might provide substantial benefits on specific campuses. Certainly, scholars such as DeCew (2003) argue that the financial benefits are real. Likewise, there is no evidence that student–faculty relations are harmed by unionization, which was a key consideration in both the Columbia University ruling and the Brown University ruling that it overturned. There are suggestions that it might actually improve relationships between students and faculty by clarifying roles and responsibilities and setting up formal routes to handle grievances. Moreover, if it is true that drawn-out, contentious organizing efforts are a source of militancy and conflict, clarity and bargaining protections could mitigate potentially problematic battles. Indeed, the existing evidence suggests that institutional resistance to bargaining is more damaging that actual bargaining.

The scarcity of research provides numerous opportunities for scholars to examine graduate student unionization, the reasons for it, and its effects. The important insider perspectives offered in strike dossiers and related writings can be supplemented by in-depth case studies of the experience of unionizing and the experiences of working in a unionized environment, for students, faculty, and administrators. Similar studies of campaigns that result in a rejection of bargaining would likewise be useful. The work on student salaries can be extended to get a better (and more up-to-date) view of wage and compensation premiums, especially when factoring in cost of living and relative rates of close peer institutions. Rhoades and Rhoads (2003) pointed to a number of lines of inquiry, including the effects of unionization on individual student identity and development, recruitment, rankings, and decision making, as well as on organizing process questions. Lee et al. (2004) called for greater consideration of disciplinary differences, socialization, and economic issues related to propensity to unionize. As with all literature on unionization, considerations of type should be woven throughout, especially considering the disparate locales of graduate student and faculty unions.

Current Understandings and Future Directions

F ACULTY AND GRADUATE student unionization are basic elements of U.S. higher education, with more than 430,000 college and university instructors operating under collectively bargained contracts and many more otherwise affiliated. From the earliest days of nonbargaining locals, through the beginnings of collective bargaining and beyond, they have also caused alarm. In 1971, for example, Central Michigan University president William B. Boyd began an early treatment of the topic: "A spectre that has been haunting higher education—the spectre of collective bargaining—is now a living presence.... The unthinkable, became thinkable, then bearable, and soon may be taken for granted" (p. 306). Boyd continued that collective bargaining was likely to spread, highlighted potential causes, and pointed to the grave dangers that it posed to academic values. He concluded, though, by noting that bargaining had also "demonstrated utility in solving some of the stickiest problems that confront university faculties and administrations" (p. 318) and called on higher education to take advantage of its benefits while avoiding its downfalls. Almost 50 years later, it is possible to look back on the results of that "spectre" to assess how it has affected higher education. Has it been a destructive force that has unsettled higher education? An effective route to improving faculty working conditions and institutional functioning? Or, as Garbarino (1974) wrote, merely "a lousy idea whose time has come?" (p. 1).

Following an overview of the history and context of faculty and graduate student unionization, this monograph has sought to answer questions about

132

the effects of faculty unionization based on the published research literature that has appeared since the rise of widespread bargaining in the late 1960s and early 1970s. It has done so through an examination of faculty attitudes toward unionization as well as the effects of tenure-line faculty, non-tenure-line faculty, and graduate student unionization. This chapter summarizes those findings before arguing for significant and substantial new research in these areas, as well as broader ones that have yet to be studied in depth but that could provide a fuller picture of higher education, instructional workers, and labor relations in the 21st century.

Overview of Existing Research

This review of the literature on unionization and bargaining has highlighted the early surge in interest in the topic, followed by increasing neglect. Perhaps, as Boyd (1971) suggested, collective bargaining has been largely taken for granted in the past few decades with rare counterexamples pushing understandings forward. As such, the following summary of findings must be understood in consideration that they are informed by some good and useful work but also that some of the findings might be less valid in the 21st century than when the issues were more fully studied in the 1970s and early 1980s.

Faculty Attitudes About Unionization

Research on attitudes and voting behaviors was especially prevalent in the first decade of unionization when it was more difficult to examine outcomes. Early studies pointed to young, low-ranked, poorly paid, politically liberal union supporters as being the most likely to support collective bargaining in hypothetical and real voting situations. In more recent years, as more advanced methods have been used, issues of satisfaction (both with pay and overall), distrust in the administration, and belief that a union could improve conditions have become much more prevalent in the literature. So, too, has the increased importance of noneconomic factors in unionization decisions. Moreover, the specific local conditions and contexts are crucial in shaping larger attitudes.

They are even more so for voting behavior as evidence reveals that those supportive of unionization broadly do not always believe it is appropriate on their own campuses and vice versa.

Compensation

Early research on compensation and tenure-line faculty, undertaken through studies matching unionized and nonunionized institutions, pointed to wage premiums among 2- and 4-year colleges. These studies, however, were questioned because of methodological concerns and some alternative findings when scholars investigated different windows in time—early union gains may have been a result of external environmental and economic factors, rather than union activities. Alternatively, they possibly showed only a short-term benefit for unionized faculty. As methods advanced and data improved, studies again showed wage premiums, especially for faculty in community colleges and comprehensive colleges and universities, although some studies still ignored cost of living, a significant shortcoming considering the differing locales of unionized and nonunionized schools. Seeking to overcome these with four iterations of NSOPF data and multiple controls, Hedrick et al. (2011) found no significant wage premium at 4-year colleges whereas Henson et al. (2012) found small significant ones at 2-year institutions. Due to limitations in NSOPF data, neither was able to consider compensation other than wages.

Potential effects on compensation extend beyond the overall salary paid to faculty to include how it is distributed and whether it promotes equity and/or creates set salary scales that inhibit merit pay. Here, too, the evidence is somewhat mixed as some union contracts include equity provisions and there is some evidence that, at unionized institutions, there is a smaller wage gap than at nonunionized institutions. At the same time, many of the contracts studied by Rhoades (1998) and others have included significant provisions for merit and retention pay, allowing administrators to provide additional wages to faculty, largely at their own discretion. Moreover, early claims that junior faculty were the ones to benefit most from unionization were countered by later evidence that collective bargaining may have stopped further dispersion in faculty salaries but did not help overcome it. Rather, bargaining could further entrench seniority and other existing rights. At the same time, research has indicated that operating under a bargained contract is associated with greater satisfaction with salary and benefits.

Tenure and Procedural Protections

The strongest and most consistent evidence of unionization's impact are in the areas of formalized tenure and promotion policies, as well as grievance procedures. Multiple studies have demonstrated that faculty have received greater written guarantees around processes and standards through collective bargaining, with the belief that such provisions can reduce arbitrariness, if not necessarily make achieving tenure easier. Union contracts have also provided more formalized retrenchment policies that have provided guidance for laying off faculty in times of financial need, enrollment shortfalls, or programmatic change. Although the research has viewed the existence of these policies as a positive, the widespread managerial discretion and low bar for retrenchment have also been criticized. Moreover, the seniority and related provisions of re- trenchment policies often work to privilege more established full-time faculty over newer and non-tenure-track faculty.

Governance and Faculty Influence

Opponents of faculty unionization have often expressed concern that bargain- ing would undermine traditional forms of shared governance, undercut the roles of faculty senates, and privilege certain union faculty voices over the in- put of the faculty as a whole. The research reviewed in this monograph does show that in select cases, faculty senates have withered or been abolished. Yet, the research is also consistent that this was most often the case at institutions that did not have strong existing mechanisms for shared governance. At those that did, senate rights were often written into contracts and otherwise bol- stered. In short, the research indicates unions provide faculty a voice where they were previously weak but do not upend existing structures if they seem to be working. Still, the broader shifts in higher education and the centraliza- tion in authority that may be related to unionization or to broader contextual factors have left some ambiguity over whether power differs at unionized and nonunionized institutions.

Climate and Collegiality

Early considerations of contentious organizing drives and bargaining relationships bore out fears that the presumed adversarial nature of bargaining would fundamentally change campus relationships, reduce collegiality, and be divisive forces. Individual cases in years since have likewise shown short-term negative effects. They have, though, been joined by reports of productive bargaining relationships and studies that have questioned whether the literature privileges the voices of those who have been most negatively affected by contentious bargaining rather than broader campus communities. Some literature has emphasized the roles of bargaining approaches taken by both unions and administrations in fostering productive climates or inhibiting them, showing that although negative climate effects can happen, they do not necessarily have to. Moreover, some studies have argued that unionization has benefited campus climates through formalization of relationships and increased transparency.

Satisfaction

The bulk of the research reviewed has indicated that unionized tenure-line faculty are not globally more satisfied than nonunionized faculty. Some has gone even further to indicate that unionized faculty are overall less satisfied with their work than nonunionized faculty, though serious causal concerns exist—dissatisfaction is associated with a desire to unionize and most studies are cross-sectional in design. Research has further indicated that unionized faculty—both tenure line and not—are more likely to be satisfied with their compensation than nonunionized faculty, but less so with other aspects of their work. To multiple scholars this has suggested a trade-off, where satisfaction is raised in some areas, lowered in others, and overall remains about the same.

Organizational Effectiveness

Very few studies have looked more broadly at the impacts of unionization on institutional effectiveness. Those that have done so have determined that there might be little. Cameron (1982), for example, found that unionized institutions were less effective than nonunionized but cautioned that his methods precluded considerations of causality. His follow-up study suggested that ineffectiveness preceded unionization but that unionization did not improve effectiveness (Cameron, 1985).

Non-Tenure-Line Faculty

The literature on the effects on non-tenure-line faculty members is likewise scarce. Some early studies included members of this population in their samples although they rarely handled their analyses separately. Those that did cautioned that the effects of unionization might be different for different faculty groups. Some pointed to gains made by instructors but others highlighted the continuation of existing privilege. Certainly, contractual language such as that favoring full-time and tenure-line faculty during retrenchment point to potential difficulties when non-tenure-line faculty are part of broader bargaining units. The considerations of part-time faculty in their own bargaining units have been more positive. They have almost uniformly found gains in security, status, wages, benefits, and protections, with only few notes of potential loss of flexibility.

Graduate Students

Because of the dual nature of their roles, collective bargaining by graduate students remains the most contentious area of instructional worker unionization in U.S. higher education. It is likewise among the least studied. Evidence points to the combination of issues that can affect attitudes about and behaviors related to unionization including wages, broader views on labor, changes in higher education writ large, increased time to degree, and social justice concerns. Perhaps the most pressing issue addressed is whether unionization would undermine faculty–student relationships. The research is clear that it has not, and some studies have suggested that it has improved them. The research is less clear on the extent of wage and compensation premiums and whether they exist at all, though numerous firsthand accounts report that they do.

Needed Additional Studies

This monograph has organized and highlighted the findings of the existing research on the effects of faculty and graduate student unionization. Yet although the general themes and findings presented here are based on the best available evidence, much more work needs to be undertaken to truly ascertain the implications of unionization in modern higher education in the United States.

With some clear exceptions, much of the work that has been undertaken has been faculty centric, examining attitudes, satisfaction, compensation, or working conditions. Although this work is plentiful, it should be renewed and extended, preferably with the type of large-scale studies that have become difficult since the end of NSOPF in 2004. Some of the best, most recent evidence comes from analyses of that data, which is now more than a dozen years old—some members of faculty unions were in high school during its last administration. Barring the renewal of truly national data, statistical considerations that pull across multiple institutions are needed; they might be aided by such things as the Higher Education Research Institute's inclusion of a question on union status in its most recent faculty survey.

These larger studies should be supplemented by in-depth case studies that provide rich detail about the experiences of all parties working in unionized institutions. Though significant insight can be garnered from the first-hand participant accounts, rigorous qualitative work can add to nuance and complicate these pieces. Cross-case and multisite studies can likewise help us understand how faculty and graduate student bargaining works both in the short term and over longer periods of time.

Some of the most useful qualitative efforts have been the large-scale contract analyses that have highlighted provisions regarding compensation (including merit pay, salary schedules, and equity), grievance procedures, property ownership, administrative discretion, and other areas. Rhoades's (1998) *Managed Professionals* remains the most significant of these for the breadth of its coverage and depth of its analysis. Yet, almost a decade ago, Twombly and Townsend (2008) praised it although warned that it was already becoming dated. Contract analyses have continued, including by Rhoades and colleagues, but large-scale, theoretically driven reconsiderations of contracts for multiple types of instructors unions are warranted.

Twombly and Townsend's (2008) comment, which was part of a larger analysis of the state of knowledge of community college faculty, further highlights the need for work that explicitly considers the full range of institutional types to try to tease out what is shared across the system and what might be most relevant in certain sectors. Although unionization is most prevalent in 2-year colleges, scholars have more often examined it at 4-year institutions. The full range of educational actors must likewise be considered—the current research overly emphasizes members of locals that include tenure-line faculty, either on their own or in broader units. The effects of unionization of both graduate students and non-tenure line, instructors are woefully understudied.

The broader organizational effects both in terms of processes and outcomes likewise beg further consideration. For example, what are the true economic effects of unionization to institutions of higher education? How does unionization affect institutional efficiency? What, if any, relationships exist between unionization and student learning outcomes, graduation rates, and student satisfaction? Does the unionization of tenure-line faculty affect the use of non-tenure-line faculty and vice versa?

As these and numerous related questions are explored, it is vitally important that the results of the studies are integrated into the scholarly literature on higher education—even a cursory examination of many of the most useful recent books on faculty, organizations, and administration will reveal that unions are largely overlooked. As such, Rhoades's (1998) critique about the lack of consideration of the unionization of instructional workers in higher education in both the literature and graduate training in the field maintains its currency. With a quarter of the faculty unionized and renewed emphases on organizing the majority who teach off the tenure track, such oversight can hardly be justified.

Looking Forward

Predicting the future of higher education is a losing proposition—even early forecasts about faculty unionization were far from prescient. Still, considering the current landscape and possible directions is potentially useful. First, there is little reason to believe that the recent efforts to organize non-tenure-line faculty in private higher education and in public higher institutions in states with enabling legislation will slow down. The conditions in which many members of this diverse group work are difficult and have both professional and personal consequences. As the research discussed here demonstrates, unionizing can make a substantial difference in these conditions, including promoting greater job security. If, as expected, non-tenure-line unionization and collective bargaining continues to spread—including through the broader coalitions of faculty that offer significant potential—the larger effect on higher education could be profound. Dobbie and Robinson's (2008) work suggested that increased union density among non-tenure-line faculty helps to mitigate the differences between their conditions and compensation and those of tenure-line faculty. They linked such changes to the reduced reliance on non-tenure-line faculty. If such is more broadly the case, the mass unionization of non-tenure-line faculty has the potential to disrupt the reorganization of the instructional workforce either by stemming or reversing the changes or by rendering them less significant.

The potential for the substantial expansion of tenure-line faculty unionization is somewhat less obvious as the *Yeshiva* decision continues to impose burdens on those who work at private colleges—the Notre Dame de Namur recognition noted at the outset of this monograph is an outlier, though one that excited union advocates. Moreover, the broader political climate does not seem conducive to the expansion of legal protections for public college faculty, tenure line, or otherwise. Indeed, the recent past has seen numerous attacks on bargaining rights for public sector unions broadly and educators specifically, with Iowa being the most recent example of a state severely restricting bargaining among college faculty and graduate students. That law, which took effect earlier this year and is currently being challenged in the courts, limits the topics that can be bargained and mandates unionized institutions to bargain only on salary. Barring significant backlashes or political shifts, there is little reason to believe that these efforts to stop unionization, which are based on ideology more than evidence such as that presented in this monograph, will subside in the near future. As such, despite recent successes organizing on some campuses and ongoing concern that higher education has been increasingly corporatized, the expansion of tenure-line faculty unions in public higher education may be constrained. It might likewise be even further confined by region.

The August 2016 NLRB ruling allowing graduate students at Columbia to collectively bargain was hailed as potentially the beginning of a new era. Students ramped up their organizing efforts and multiple institutions held representation elections in the most recent academic year. Yet not all of those efforts were successful; the results of several remain contested as of this writing. More significantly, there is widespread concern among union advocates that the current presidential administration will reshape the NLRB in ways that promote business interests over workers' rights. As the conflicting rulings over the past half-century have shown, graduate student rights can be quickly removed. Indeed, some have argued that universities are intentionally delaying negotiations, hoping that the ruling is reversed before they agree to contracts with their graduate student employees.

These highly charged battles over union rights make sense considering the polarized political landscape, historic views of a professional faculty, and the pressures on modern higher education. They are less logical in light of the existing research on unionization and instructional workers. As has been repeatedly highlighted, much is unknown about the broad effects of unionization in higher education in the modern era, including the differential effects on different categories of workers and different institutional types and sectors. But just as Baldridge et al. (1981) concluded in an AAHE-ERIC/Higher Education Research Report more than 35 years ago, unions have not brought about the "revolutionary change" (p. 46) that proponents hoped for and detractors feared. Unions have offered somewhat positive effects for faculty and graduate students in some areas, without fundamentally unsettling the structure of higher education or preventing increased corporatization and substantial managerial discretion. Even the potentially negative effects on things such as climate and collegiality have been avoided at some institutions or have faded over time; some have suggested that the assumption of adversarial relations is partly responsible for their existence. Moreover, it is quite reasonable to question whether the battles over unionization in statehouses and on individual campuses are more divisive than actual collective bargaining. As with much of the ground covered here, though, more research is needed to assess whether such is the case.

References

AAUP. (2005). Academic unionism statement. Retrieved from https://www.aaupcbc.org/academic-unionism-statement

Adler, D. L. (1977). *Governance and collective bargaining in four-year institutions, 1970–1977*. Washington, DC: Academic Collective Bargaining Information Service.

AFT Inventories, Part I. (1947–1951). Archive of Labor and Urban Affairs, Wayne State University (Series IV, Box 35, Folder "Association of Tri-State College Professors"), Detroit, MI.

Ali, S. M., & Karim, A. R. (1992). An empirical examination of determinants of faculty attitude toward collective bargaining. *Journal of Collective Negotiations in the Public Sector, 21*, 79–91.

Alleman, N. F., Cliburn Allen, C., & Haviland, D. (in press). Collegiality and the collegium in an era of faculty differentiation *[ASHE Higher Education Report]*. San Francisco, CA: Jossey Bass.

Allen, R. E., & Keaveny, T. J. (1981). Correlates of university faculty interest in unionization: A replication and extension. *Journal of Applied Psychology, 66*, 582–589.

Ambash, J. W. (2016, September 7). NLRB's graduate-assistant ruling: Bad news for administrators and students. *Chronicle of Higher Education*. Retrieved from http://www.chronicle.com/article/NLRB-s-Graduate-Assistant/237714

Andes, J. (1974). *Developing trends in the content of collective bargaining contracts in higher education*. Washington, DC: Academic Collective Bargaining Information Service.

Andes, J. (1982). A decade of development in higher education collective bargaining: Changes in contract content. *Journal of Collective Negotiations in the Public Sector, 11*, 285–295.

Arnold, G. B. (2000). *The politics of faculty unionization: The experience of three New England universities*. Westport, CT: Bergin & Garvey.

Ashraf, J. (1992). Do unions affect faculty salaries? *Economics of Education Review, 11*, 219–223.

Ashraf, J. (1997). The effect of unions on professors' salaries: The evidence over twenty years. *Journal of Labor Research, 18,* 439–450.

Ashraf, J. (1998). Collective bargaining and compensation at public junior colleges. *Journal of Collective Negotiations in the Public Sector, 27,* 393–399.

Ashraf, J. (1999). Faculty unionism in the 1990s: A comparison of public and private universities. *Journal of Collective Negotiations in the Public Sector, 28,* 303–310.

Ashraf, J., & Aydin, R. (2009). Collective bargaining and academic compensation: Evidence in the 21st century. *Southwest Business and Economics Journal, 17,* 15–21.

Ashraf, J., & Williams, M. F. (2008). The effect of faculty unions on salaries: Some recent evidence. *Journal of Collective Negotiations, 32,* 141–150.

Aussieker, B. (1975a). Community colleges without community. In Carnegie Commission on Higher Education (Ed.), *Faculty bargaining: Change and conflict* (pp. 179–212). New York, NY: McGraw-Hill.

Aussieker, B. (1975b). Student involvement with collective bargaining. *Journal of Higher Education, 46,* 533–547.

Bacharach, S. B., Schmidle, T. P., & Bauer, S. C. (1987). Higher education. In D. B. Lipsky & C. B. Dunn (Eds.), *Collective bargaining in American industry: Contemporary perspectives and future directions* (pp. 225–264). Lexington, MA: Lexington Books.

Bain, T. (1976). Collective bargaining and wages in higher education: The case of CUNY (New York City). *Journal of Collective Negotiations in the Public Sector, 5,* 207–214.

Baker, H. K. (1984a). The economic impact of collective bargaining across academic ranks. *Journal of Collective Negotiations in the Public Sector, 13,* 339–349.

Baker, H. K. (1984b). The short- and long-term effects of collective bargaining on faculty compensation. *Journal of Collective Negotiations in the Public Sector, 13,* 235–250.

Baldridge, J. V., Curtis, D. V., Ecker, G., & Riley, G. L. (1978). *Policy making and effective leadership: A national study of academic management.* San Francisco, CA: Jossey-Bass.

Baldridge, J. V., & Kemerer, F. R. (1976). Academic senates and faculty collective bargaining. *Journal of Higher Education, 47,* 391–411.

Baldridge, J. V., Kemerer, F. R., & Associates. (1981). Assessing the impact of faculty collective bargaining *[AAHE-ERIC/Higher Education Research Report, 10(8)].* Washington, DC: American Association for Higher Education.

Baldridge, J. V., & Tierney, M. L. (1979). *New approaches to management: Creating practical systems of management information and management by objectives.* San Francisco, CA: Jossey-Bass.

Baldwin, R. G., & Wawrzynski, M. R. (2011). Contingent faculty as teachers what we know; what we need to know. *American Behavioral Scientist, 55,* 1485–1509.

Balkin, D. B. (1989). Union influence on faculty satisfaction with compensation and resources. *Journal of Collective Negotiations in the Public Sector, 18,* 315–326.

Barba, W. C. (1994a). The graduate student employee union in SUNY: A history. *Journal for Higher Education Management, 10*(1), 39–47.

Barba, W. C. (1994b). The unionization movement: An analysis of graduate student employee contracts. *NACUBO Business Officer, 27*(5), 35–43.

Barbezat, D. A. (1989). The effect of collective bargaining on salaries in higher education. *Industrial and Labor Relations Review, 42,* 443–455.

Bayer, A. E. (1970). *College and university faculty: A statistical description [ACE Reports, 5(5)]*. Washington, DC: American Council on Education. Retrieved from ERIC database. (ED042425)

Bayer, A. E. (1973). *Teaching faculty in academe: 1972–1973 [ACE Reports, 8(2)].*: Washington, DC: American Council on Education. Retrieved from ERIC database. (ED080517)

Beauvais, L. L., Scholl, R. W., & Cooper, E. A. (1991). Dual commitment among unionized faculty: A longitudinal investigation. *Human Relations, 44*, 175–192.

Begin, J. P. (1974). Faculty governance and collective bargaining: An early appraisal. *Journal of Higher Education, 45*, 582–593.

Begin, J. P. (1977). *Due process and collegiality under faculty grievance mechanisms: The case of Rutgers University.* New Brunswick, NJ: Rutgers University, Institute of Management and Labor Relations.

Begin, J. P. (1978). Grievance mechanics and faculty collegiality: The Rutgers case. *Industrial and Labor Relations Review, 31*, 295–309.

Begin, J. P. (1979). Faculty bargaining and faculty reward systems. In D. R. Lewis & W. E. Becker, Jr. (Eds.), *Academic rewards in higher education* (pp. 245–298). Cambridge, MA: Ballinger.

Begin, J. P., Settle, T., & Alexander, P. (1977). *Academic bargaining: Origins and growth.* New Brunswick, NJ: Rutgers University, Institute of Management and Labor Relations.

Benedict, M. E. (2007). The effect of unionization on faculty salaries, 1978–1996: A test of empirical methods. *Journal of Collective Negotiations, 31*, 251–274.

Benedict, M. E., & Wilder, L. (1999). Unionization and tenure and rank outcomes in Ohio universities. *Journal of Labor Research, 20*, 185–201.

Benjamin, E., & Mauer, M. (Eds.). (2006). *Academic collective bargaining.* New York, NY: American Association of University Professors; Washington, DC: Modern Language Association.

Bernhardt, R. G. (1977). Why collective bargaining in higher education. *Research in Higher Education, 7*, 79–95.

Berry, J. (2005). *Reclaiming the ivory tower: Organizing adjuncts to change higher education.* New York, NY: Monthly Review Press.

Berry, J., & Savarese, M. (2012). *Directory of U.S. faculty contracts and bargaining agents in institutions of higher education.* New York, NY: National Center for the Study of Collective Bargaining in Higher Education and the Professions, Hunter College of the City University of New York.

Bigoness, W. J. (1978). Correlates of faculty attitudes toward collective bargaining. *Journal of Applied Psychology, 63*, 228–233.

Bigoness, W. J., & Tosi, H. L. (1984). Correlates of voting behavior in a union decertification election. *Academy of Management Journal, 27*, 654–659.

Birnbaum, R. (1974). Unionization and faculty compensation. *Educational Record, 55*, 29–33.

Birnbaum, R. (1976). Unionization and faculty compensation: Part II. *Educational Record, 57*, 116–118.

Birnbaum, R. (1977, April). Compensation and academic bargaining: New findings and new directions. In A. Levenstein (Ed.), *Collective bargaining and the future of higher education. Proceedings, fifth annual conference* (pp. 64–73). New York, NY: National Center for the Study of Collective Bargaining in Higher Education.

Birnbaum, R. (1984). The effects of a neutral third party on academic bargaining relationships and campus climate. *Journal of Higher Education, 55,* 719–734.

Birnbaum, R. & Inman, D. (1984). The relationship of academic bargaining to changes in campus climate. *Journal of Higher Education, 55,* 609–620.

Blader, S. (2007). What leads organizational members to collectivize? *Organization Science, 18,* 108–126.

Bognanno, M. F., Estenson, D.L., & Suntrup, E. L. (1978). Union-management contracts in higher education. *Industrial Relations, 17,* 189–203.

Bornheimer, D. G. (1985). Conditions influencing faculty voting in collective bargaining elections. *Research in Higher Education, 22,* 291–305.

Borstoff, P. C., Nye, D. L., & Field, H. S (1994). Correlates of collective bargaining support in a right-to-work state: A study of university professors. *Journal of Collective Negotiations in the Public Sector, 23,* 15–26.

Boyd, W. B. (1971). Collective bargaining in academe: Causes and consequences. *Liberal Education, 17,* 306–318.

Breitzer, S. R. (2003). More than academic: Labor consciousness and the rise of UE Local 896-COGS. In D. M. Herman & J. M. Schmid (Eds.), *Cogs in the classroom factory: The changing identity of academic labor* (pp. 71–90). Westport, CT: Praeger.

Broad, M. C. (2016, September 9). NLRB's Columbia decision masks new federal encroachment on campuses. *Huffington Post.* Retrieved from http://www.huffingtonpost.com/molly-corbett-broad/nlrbs-columbia-decision-m_b_11936612.html

Brown, W. R. (1982). *Academic politics.* Tuscaloosa, AL: University of Alabama Press.

Brown, W. W., & Stone, C. C. (1977a). Academic unions in higher education: Impacts on faculty salary, compensation and promotions. *Economic Inquiry, 17,* 385–396.

Brown, W. W., & Stone, C. C. (1977b). Collective bargaining and faculty compensation revisited. *Sociology of Education, 50,* 310–314.

Brown, W. W., & Stone, C. C. (1977c). Faculty compensation under unionization: Current research methods and findings. In A. Levenstein (Ed.), *Collective bargaining and the future of higher education. Proceedings, fifth annual conference* (pp. 74–91). New York, NY: National Center for the Study of Collective Bargaining in Higher Education.

Browne, M. J., & Trieschmann, J. S. (1991). Salary and benefit compensation at American research universities. *Journal of Risk and Insurance, 58,* 513–524.

Bucklew, N., Houghton, J. D., & Ellison, C. N. (2013). Faculty union and faculty senate coexistence: A review of the impact of academic collective bargaining on traditional academic governance. *Labor Studies Journal, 37,* 373–390.

Cain, B., Budke, J. M., Wood, K. J., Sweeney, N. T., & Schwessinger, B. (2014). Point of view: How postdocs benefit from building a union. *eLife.* Retrieved from https://doi.org/10.7554/eLife.05614

Cain, T. R. (2010). The first attempts to unionize the faculty. *Teachers College Record, 112,* 875–913.

Cain, T. R. (2012a). *Establishing academic freedom: Politics, principles, and the development of core values.* New York, NY: Palgrave Macmillan.

Cain, T. R. (2012b). "Only organized effort will find the way out!": Faculty unionization at Howard University, 1918–1950. *Perspectives on the History of Higher Education, 29,* 113–150.

Cain, T. R. (2012c). Unionised faculty and the political left: Communism and the American Federation of Teachers on the eve of World War II. *History of Education, 41*, 515–535.

Camacho, S., & Rhoads, R. A. (2015). Breaking the silence: The unionization of postdoctoral workers at the University of California. *Journal of Higher Education, 86*, 295–325.

Cameron, K. (1982). The relationship between faculty unionism and organizational effectiveness. *Academy of Management Journal, 25*, 6–24.

Cameron, K. (1985). Investigating the causal association between unionism and organizational effectiveness. *Research in Higher Education, 23*, 387–411.

Carey, S. F. (1978). Reasons why faculty members accept or reject unions in higher education: The University of Massachusetts experience. *Journal of Law and Education, 7*, 79–86.

Carlton, P. W. (1995). Interest-based collective bargaining at Youngstown State University: A fresh organizational approach. *Journal of Collective Negotiations in the Public Sector, 24*, 337–347.

Carnegie Commission on Higher Education. (1973). *Governance of higher education: Six priority problems*. New York, NY: McGraw-Hill.

Carr, R. K., & Van Eyck, D. K. (1973). *Collective bargaining comes to the campus*. Washington, DC: American Council on Education.

Cassell, M., & Halesah, O. (2014). The impact of unionization on university performance. *Journal of Collective Bargaining in the Academy, 6*(3), 1–23. Retrieved from http://thekeep.eiu.edu/jcba/vol6/iss1/3

Castro, C. R. (2000). Community college faculty satisfaction and the faculty union. In L. S. Hagedorn (Ed.), *New Directions for Institutional Research: No. 105. What contributes to job satisfaction among faculty and staff* (pp. 45–55). San Francisco, CA: Jossey-Bass.

Chandler, M. K., & Julius, D. (1979). *Faculty vs. administration: Rights issues in academic collective bargaining*. Retrieved from ERIC database. (ED201258)

Chandler, M. K., & Julius, D. (1985). *A study of governance in the unionized two-year institution*. Retrieved from ERIC database. (ED266821)

Chandler, M. K., & Julius, D. (1987). Determining outcomes of collective bargaining in two-year institutions—Part 1. *Community/Junior College Quarterly of Research and Practice, 11*, 203–226.

Chandler, M. K., & Julius, D. (1988). Determining outcomes of collective bargaining in two-year institutions—Part 2. *Community/Junior College Quarterly of Research and Practice, 12*, 1–20.

Chanvisanuruk, J., Rubin B. M., Kearns, A., Rubin, R. S., & McCoy, K. (2007). Graduate student employees and their propensity to unionize: Part I, A heuristic approach. *Journal of Collective Negotiations, 31*, 173–182.

Christenson, A. (1971). Collective bargaining in a university: The University of Wisconsin and the Teaching Assistants Association. *Wisconsin Law Review, 210*, 210–228.

Coalition on the Academic Workforce. (2012). *A portrait of part-time faculty members: A summary of findings on part-time faculty respondents to the Coalition on the Academic Workforce survey of contingent faculty members and instructors*. Retrieved from http://www.academicworkforce.org/CAW_portrait_2012.pdf

Columbia University, 364 NLRB No. 90 (2016, August 23).

Craig, J. S. (1986). *Graduate student unionism: The teaching assistants association at the University of Wisconsin, 1970–1980* (Doctoral dissertation). Retrieved from ProQuest Dissertations. (8702298)

Crisci, P. E., Fisher, M. L., Blixt, S. L., & Brewer, A. M. (1990). Nursing faculty attitudes toward collective bargaining for nursing faculty and for nurses in the service setting. *Journal of Collective Negotiations in the Public Sector, 19*, 29–47.

Cross, J. G., & Goldenberg, E. N. (2009). *Off-track profs: Nontenured teachers in higher education*. Cambridge, MA: MIT Press.

Curtis, J. W. (2011). *Persistent inequity: Gender and academic employment.* Paper prepared for "New Voices in Pay Equity": An event for equal pay day. Retrieved from https://www.aaup.org/NR/rdonlyres/08E023AB-E6D8-4DBD-99A0-24E5EB73A760/0/persistent_inequity.pdf

Czitrom, D. (1997). Reeling in the years: Looking back on the TAA. In C. Nelson (Ed.), *Will teach for food: Academic labor in crisis* (pp. 216–228). Minneapolis, MN: University of Minnesota Press.

Dallinger, J. M., & Beveridge, M. D. (1993). *Faculty satisfaction with the influence of a union and the administration on aspects of academic jobs.* Paper presented at the annual meeting of the Association for Institutional Research, Chicago, IL. Retrieved from ERIC database. (ED371655)

Dayal, S. (1982). Faculty unionism and bargaining attitudes and perceptions: A case study of Central Michigan University. *Labor Law Journal, 33*, 554–560.

Dayal, S. (1986). Faculty unionism and bargaining goals: Evidence from the public sector. *Journal of Collective Negotiations in the Public Sector, 15*, 347–356.

Dayal, S. (1992). White-collar union-management relations: A study of university professors. *Journal of Collective Negotiations in the Public Sector, 21*, 239–254.

DeCew, J. W. (2003). *Unionization in the academy: Visions and realities.* Lanham, MD: Rowman & Littlefield.

Decker, R., Hines, E., & Brickell, J. (1985). Assessing the impact of collective bargaining in Illinois community colleges. *Journal of Collective Negotiations in the Public Sector, 14*, 329–342.

Deckop, J. R., McClendon, J. A., & Harris-Pereles, K. L. (1993). The effect of strike militancy intentions and general union attitudes on the organizational citizenship behavior of university faculty. *Employee Responsibilities & Rights Journal, 6*, 85–97.

Dennison, G. M., Drummond, M. E., & Hobgood, W. P. (1997). Collaborative bargaining in public universities. *Negotiation Journal, 13*(1), 61–81.

Dobbie, D., & Robinson, I. (2008). Reorganizing higher education in the United States and Canada: The erosion of tenure and the unionization of contingent faculty. *Labor Studies Journal, 33*(2), 117–140.

Dobson, B. (2016, August 10). TCC faculty overwhelmingly votes to unionize. *Tallahassee Democrat.* Retrieved from http://www.tallahassee.com/story/news/2016/08/04/tcc-faculty-overwhelmingly-votes-unionize/88118794/

Douglas, J. M. (1979). The impact of collective bargaining on governance. PERS Information Bulletin, 2(1). Retrieved from ERIC database. (ED171223)

Douglas, J. M. (1988). Professors on strike: And analysis of two decades of faculty work stoppage—1966–1985. *Labor Lawyer, 4*(1), 87–101.

Douglas, J. M. (1990). The impact of NLRB v. Yeshiva University on faculty unionism at public colleges and universities. *Journal of Collective Negotiations in the Public Sector, 19*, 1–28.

Douglas, J. M. (with DeBona, L.). (1984). *Directory of faculty contracts and bargaining agents in higher education and the professions* (Vol. 10). New York, NY: National Center for the Study of Collective Bargaining in Higher Education and the Professions, Baruch College of the City University of New York.

Driscoll, J. W. (1978). Attitudes of college faculties toward unions: Two case studies. *Monthly Labor Review, 101*(5), 42–45.

Drummond, M. E., & Reitsch, A. (1995). The relationship between shared governance models and faculty and administrator attitudes. *Journal for Higher Education Management, 11*(1), 49–58.

Dubin, R., & Beisse, F. (1967). The assistant: Academic subaltern. *Administrative Science Quarterly, 11*, 521–547.

Duncan, K. C., Krall, L., Maxcy, J. G., & Prus, M. J. (2004). Faculty productivity, seniority, and salary compression. *Eastern Economic Journal, 30*, 293–310.

Dworkin, J. B., & Lee, D. (1985). Faculty intentions to unionize: Theory and evidence. *Research in Higher Education, 23*, 375–386.

Dyson, W. (1941). *Howard University: The capstone of Negro education*. Washington, DC: Howard University Graduate School.

Eagan, M. K., & Jaeger, A. J. (2009). Effects of exposure to part-time faculty on community college transfer. *Research in Higher Education, 50*, 168–188.

Editorial Board. (2016, August 24). Unions in the ivory tower. *New York Times*. Retrieved from http://www.nytimes.com/2016/08/25/opinion/unions-in-the-ivory-tower.html?action=click&pgtype=Homepage&clickSource=story-heading&module=opinion-c-col-left-region&region=opinion-c-col-left-region&WT.nav=opinion-c-col-left-region

Ehrenberg, R. G., Klaff, D. B., Kezsbom, A. T., & Nagowski, M. P. (2004). Collective bargaining in American higher education. In R. G. Ehrenberg (Ed.), *Governing academia* (pp. 209–295). Ithaca, NY: Cornell University Press.

Ehrenberg, R. G., & Zhang, L. (2005). Do tenured and tenure-track faculty matter? *Journal of Human Resources, 45*, 647–659.

Eidlin, B. (2016, June 18). The house that Reuther built. *Jacobin*. Retrieved from https://www.jacobinmag.com/2016/06/uaw-academic-workers-colleges-union-walter-reuther-treaty-detroit/

Elmuti, D., & Kathawala, Y. (1991). Full-time university faculty members' perception of unionization impact on overall compensation dimensions. *Journal of Research and Development in Education, 24*(2), 9–15.

Farber, H. S., & Saks, D. H. (1980). Why workers want unions: The role of relative wages and job characteristics. *Journal of Political Economy, 88*, 349–369.

Feinsinger, N. P., & Roe, E. J. (1971). The University of Wisconsin, Madison Campus—TAA dispute of 1969–70: A case study. *Wisconsin Law Review, 229*, 229–274.

Feuille, P., & Blandin, J. (1974). Faculty job satisfaction and bargaining sentiments: A case study. *Academy of Management Journal, 17*, 678–692.

Feuille, P., & Blandin, J. (1976). University faculty and attitudinal militancy toward the employment relationship. *Sociology of Education, 49*, 139–145.

Finkelstein, M. J., Conley, V. M., & Schuster, J. H. (2016). *The faculty factor: Reassessing the American academy in a turbulent era*. Baltimore: Johns Hopkins University Press.

Finley, C. (1991). The relationship between unionization and job satisfaction among two-year college faculty. *Community College Review, 2*, 53–61.

Fiorito, J., Padavic, I., & Russell, Z. A. (2014). Union beliefs and activism: A research note. *Journal of Labor Research, 35*, 346–357.

Fiorito, J., Tope, D., Steinberg, P. E., Padavic, I., & Murphy, C. E. (2011). Lay activism and activism intentions in a faculty union: An exploratory study. *Labor Studies Journal, 36*, 483–507.

Flaherty, C. (2013, July 26). Union raises for adjuncts. *Inside Higher Ed.* Retrieved from https://www.insidehighered.com/news/2013/07/26/adjunct-union-contracts-ensure-real-gains-including-better-pay

Flaherty, C. (2014, November 25). Winning raises without contracts? *Inside Higher Ed.* Retrieved from https://www.insidehighered.com/news/2014/11/25/union-activity-leads-gains-adjuncts-even-when-bids-fail-or-stall

Flaherty, C. (2015, February 9). 15K per course? *Inside Higher Ed.* Retrieved from https://www.insidehighered.com/news/2015/02/09/union-sets-aspirational-goal-adjunct-pay

Flaherty, C. (2016a, August 24). NLRB: Graduate students at private universities may unionize. Inside Higher Ed. Retrieved from https://www.insidehighered.com/news/2016/08/24/nlrb-says-graduate-students-private-universities-may-unionize

Flaherty, C. (2016b, June 1). Notre Dame de Namur recognizes tenured faculty union. *Inside Higher Ed.* Retrieved from https://www.insidehighered.com/quicktakes/2016/06/01/notre-dame-de-namur-recognizes-tenured-faculty-union

Flango, V. E. (1975). Faculty attitudes and the election of a bargaining agent in the Pennsylvania State College System–I. *Journal of Collective Negotiations in the Public Sector, 4*, 157–174.

Flango, V. E., & Brumbaugh, R. B. (1972). *Preference for bargaining representative: Some empirical findings.* Kutztown, PA: Center for Educational Change Through Organizational and Technological Development, Kutztown State College. Retrieved from ERIC database. (ED071158)

Freeman, R. B. (1978). Should we organize? Effects of faculty unionism on academic compensation (Working Paper No. 301). Cambridge, MA: National Bureau of Economic Research. Retrieved from http://www.nber.org/papers/w0301

Gable, M., & Coolsen, J. (1975). Faculty attitudes toward job actions, the union, and the administration: The effect of unionization at a college campus. *Journal of Collective Negotiations in the Public Sector, 4*, 309–318.

Garbarino, J. W. (1972). Faculty unionism: From theory to practice. *Industrial Relations, 11*(1), 1–17.

Garbarino, J. W. (1974). Faculty unionism in the west. *Industrial Relations, 13*, 1–4.

Garbarino, J. W. (with Aussieker, B.). (1975). *Faculty bargaining: Change and conflict.* New York, NY: McGraw-Hill.

Garbarino, J. W., & Lawler, J. (1979). Faculty union activity in higher education. *Industrial Relations, 18*, 244–246.

Garcia, E. H. (1975). Community college labor contracts and issues: An analysis of 64 agreements. *Journal of Collective Negotiations in the Public Sector, 4*, 83–100.

Gehrke, S. J., & Kezar, A. (2015). Supporting non-tenure-track at 4-year colleges and universities: A national study of deans' values and decisions. *Educational Policy, 29*, 926–960.

Gershenfeld, W. J., & Mortimer, K. P. (1979). Faculty collective bargaining activity in Pennsylvania, 1970–75. *Journal of Collective Negotiations in the Public Sector, 8*, 131–149.

Gilmore, C. B. (1981). The impact of faculty collective bargaining on the management of public higher educational institutions. *Journal of Collective Negotiations in the Public Sector, 10*, 145–152.

Goeddeke, F. X., Jr., & Kammeyer-Mueller, J. D. (2010). Perceived support in a dual organizational environment: Union participation in a university setting. *Journal of Organizational Behavior, 31*, 65–83.

Goldey, G. T., Swank, E., Hardesty, C., & Swain, R. (2008). The determinants of union attitudes among community college professors. *Journal of Collective Negotiations, 32*, 261–277.

Gomez-Mejia, L., & Balkin, D. (1984). Faculty satisfaction with pay and other job dimensions under union and non-union conditions. *Academy of Management Journal, 27*, 591–602.

Goodwin, H. I. (Ed.). (1977). *Collective bargaining perspectives. Part-time faculty.* Retrieved from ERIC database. Morgantown, WV: Department of Educational Administration, West Virginia University. (ED145753)

Goodwin, H. I., & Andes, J. (1972). Contract trends in higher education collective bargaining. *Journal of Collective Negotiations in the Public Sector, 1*, 299–308.

Gordon, M. E., & Denisi, A. S. (1995). A re-examination of the relationship between union membership and job satisfaction. *Industrial and Labor Relations Review, 48*, 226–236.

Graf, L. A., Hemmasi, M., Newgren, K. E., & Nielsen, W. R. (1994). Profiles of those who support collective bargaining in institutions of higher learning and why: An empirical examination. *Journal of Collective Negotiations in the Public Sector, 23*, 151–162.

Greenberg, I. (2014). Impossible unity: Adjuncts and tenure-track faculty. *New Labor Forum, 23*(1), 11–13.

Gress, J. R. (1976). Predicting faculty attitude toward collective bargaining. *Research in Higher Education, 4*, 247–256.

Gross, A. (2006). Campus union coalitions and the corporate university: Organizing the University of California. In E. Benjamin & M. Mauer (Eds.), *Academic collective bargaining* (pp. 332–348). Washington, DC: Modern Language Association & American Association of University Professors.

Guthrie-Morse, B., Leslie, L. L., & Hu, T.-W. (1981). Assessing the impact of faculty unions: The financial implications of collective bargaining. *Journal of Higher Education, 52*, 237–255.

Haehn, J. O. (1970). *A survey of faculty and administrators attitudes on collective bargaining. A report to the Academic Senate, California State Colleges.* Sacramento: Academic Senate of the California State Colleges.

Hagengruber, D. L. (1978). Reasons why faculty members accept or reject unions in higher education: The University of Wisconsin experience. *Journal of Law and Education, 7*(1), 53–78.

Hammer, T. H., & Berman, M. (1981). The role of noneconomic factors in faculty union voting. *Journal of Applied Psychology, 66*, 415–421.

Hansen, W. L. (1988). Merit pay and higher education. In D. W. Breneman & T. I. K. Youn, *Academic labor markets and careers* (pp. 114–137). New York, NY: Falmer Press.

Hayden, G. M. (2001). "The university works because we do": Collective bargaining rights for graduate students. *Fordham Law Review, 69*, 1233–1264.

Hedgepeth, R. C. (1974). Consequences of collective bargaining in higher education: An exploratory analysis. *Journal of Higher Education, 45*, 691–705.

Hedrick, D. W., Henson, S. E., Krieg, J. M., & Wassell, C. S., Jr. (2011). Is there really a faculty union salary premium? *Industrial and Labor Relations Review, 64*, 558–575.

Hemmasi, M., & Graf, L. A. (1993). Determinants of faculty voting behavior in union representation elections: A multivariate model. *Journal of Management, 19*, 13–22.

Henson, S. E., Krieg, J. M., Wassell, C. S., Jr., & Hedrick, D. W. (2012). Collective bargaining and community college faculty: What is the wage impact? *Journal of Labor Research, 33*, 104–117.

Herbert, W. A. (2016). The winds of changes shift: An analysis of recent growth in bargaining units and representation efforts in higher education. *Journal of Collective Bargaining in the Academy, 8*. Retrieved from http://thekeep.eiu.edu/jcba/vol8/iss1/1/

Herman, D. M., & Schmid, J. M. (2003). *Cogs in the classroom factory: The changing identity of academic labor.* Westport, CT: Praeger.

Herziger, W. A. (1967, June 29) [Letter to Hervey A. Juris]. Wisconsin Historical Society (U.S. Mss. 77a, Box 2, Folder 4), Madison, WI.

Hewitt, G. J. (2000). Graduate student employee collective bargaining and the educational relationship between faculty and graduate students. *Journal of Collective Negotiations in the Public Sector, 29*, 153–166.

Hicks, S. (2014). Post-recession CBAs: A study of wage increases in the agreements of four state-wide faculty unions. *Journal of Collective Bargaining in the Academy, 6*. Retrieved from http://thekeep.eiu.edu/jcba/vol6/iss1/4

Hill, M. D. (1982) Variations in job satisfaction among higher education faculty in unionized and nonunionized institutions in Pennsylvania. *Journal of Collective Negotiations in the Public Sector, 11*, 165–179.

Hoeller, K. (2009). The academic labor system of faculty apartheid. In K. Hoeller (Ed.), *Equality for contingent faculty: Overcoming the two-tier system* (pp. 116–155). Nashville, TN: Vanderbilt University Press.

Hoeller, K. (2010, December 9). We need an adjunct union. *Inside Higher Ed.* Retrieved from https://www.insidehighered.com/views/2010/12/09/we-need-adjunct-union

Hoffman, E. (2006). From cynicism to commitment: The impact of collective bargaining and campus climate on contingent faculty members. In E. Benjamin & M. Mauer (Eds.), *Academic collective bargaining* (pp. 23–51). Washington, DC: Modern Language Association & American Association of University Professors.

Hoffman, E., & Hess, J. (2009). Organizing for equality with the two-tier system: The experience of the California Faculty Association. In K. Hoeller (Ed.), *Equality for contingent faculty: Overcoming the two-tier system* (pp. 9–27). Nashville, TN: Vanderbilt University Press.

Holsinger, N. (2008). "Union yes" at a public ivy: Predictors of faculty voting intentions at the University of Vermont. *Labor Studies Journal, 33*, 288–308.

Hu, T. W., & Leslie, L. (1982). The effects of collective bargaining on college faculty salaries and compensation. *Applied Economics, 14*, 269–277.

Hurd, R., & Foerster, A. (with Johnson, B. H). (1996). *Directory of faculty contracts and bargaining agents in institutions of higher education* (Vol. 22). New York, NY: National Center for the Study of Collective Bargaining in Higher Education and the Professions, Baruch College of the City University of New York. Retrieved from ERIC database. (ED409813)

Hutchens, N. H., & Hutchens, M. B. (2003/2004). Catching the union bug: Graduate student employees and unionization. *Gonzaga Law Review, 39*, 105–130.

Hutcheson, P. A. (2000). *A professional professoriate: Unionization, bureaucratization, and the AAUP*. Nashville, TN: Vanderbilt University Press.

Ingerman, S. (1965). Employed graduate students organize at Berkeley. *Industrial Relations, 5*, 145–150.

Ito, H., & Masoner, M. (1980). Compensation gains in higher education: A reexamination. *Sociology of Education, 53*, 60–64.

Jackson, P. I., & Clark, R. D. (1987). Collective bargaining and faculty compensation: Faculty as a new working class. *Sociology of Education, 60*, 242–256.

Jacobs, J. A., & Winslow, S. E. (2004). Overworked faculty: Job stress and family demands. *Annals of the American Academy of Political and Social Science, 596*, 104–129.

Johnson, B., & McCarthy, T. (2000). Graduate student organizing at Yale and the future of the labor movement in higher education. *Social Policy, 30*(4), 11–18.

Johnson, K. Q., & Entin, J. (2000). Graduate employee organizing and the corporate university. *New Labor Forum, 6*, 99–107.

Johnson, M. D., & Mortimer, K. P. (1977). Faculty bargaining and the politics of retrenchment in Pennsylvania state colleges, 1971–1976. University Park, PA: Pennsylvania State University, Center for the Study of Higher Education.

Johnstone, R. L. (1981). *The scope of faculty collective bargaining: An analysis of faculty union agreements at four-year institutions of higher education*. Westport, CT: Greenwood Press.

Julius, D. J. (1994). Assessing the impact of employee unionization in community and junior colleges. In A. M. Hoffman, & D. J. Julius (Eds.), *Managing community and junior colleges: Perspectives for the next century* (pp. 111–146). Washington, DC: College and University Personnel Association.

Julius, D. J., & Chandler, M. K. (1989). Academic bargaining agents in higher education: Do their achievements matter? *Journal of Collective Negotiations in the Public Sector, 18*, 9–58.

Julius, D. J., & DiGiovanni, N., Jr. (2013). What's ahead in faculty collective bargaining? The new and the déjà vu. *Journal of Collective Bargaining in the Academy, 4*. Retrieved from http://thekeep.eiu.edu/jcba/vol4/iss1/5

Julius, D. J., & Gumport, P. J. (2002). Graduate student unionization: Catalysts and consequences. *Review of Higher Education, 26*, 187–216.

Karim, A. R., & Ali, S. M. (1993). Demographic differences and faculty attitude toward collective bargaining. *Journal of Collective Negotiations in the Public Sector, 22*, 87–97.

Karim, A., & Rassuli, A. (1996). Attitude of faculty toward unionization: Evidence from a southwestern state. *Journal of Collective Negotiations in the Public Sector, 25*, 311–321.

Katchanovski, I., Rothman, S., & Nevitte, N. (2011). Attitudes towards faculty unions and collective bargaining in American and Canadian Universities. *Relations Industrielles/Industrial Relations, 66*, 349–373.

Kater, S., & Levin, J. S. (2005). Shared governance in community colleges in the global economy. *Community College Journal of Research and Practice, 29*, 1–23.

Katsinas, S. G., Ogun, J. A., & Bray, N. J. (2016). *Monetary compensation of full-time faculty at American public regional universities: The impact of geography and the existence of collective bargaining*. Paper presented at the 43rd Annual Conference of the National Center for the Study of Collective Bargaining in

Higher Education and the Professions. Retrieved from http://www.chronicle.com/
items/biz/pdf/2016-4-3%20Compensation%20of%20FT%20faculty%20at%20Regional
%20Universities-Katsinas%20Ogun%20and%20Bray.pdf

Kazlow, C., & Giaquinta, J. (1977). Tenure, support of collective bargaining, and unionism in higher education: Some challenging findings. *Research in Higher Education*, 6,
45–63.

Kearney, R. C., & Morgan, D. R. (1977). Collective bargaining and faculty compensation: A
comparative analysis. *Sociology of Education*, 50, 315–317.

Kelley, L. (1979). Leadership, pay, and promotion as predictors of choice of bargaining unit in
a university. *Journal of Collective Negotiations in the Public Sector*, 8, 291–298.

Kelley, L., & Edge, A. G. (1976). An assessment of attitudinal change toward collective bargaining of the University of Hawaii faculty: 1972–1974. *Journal of Collective Negotiations
in the Public Sector*, 5, 349–359.

Kemerer, F. R. (1983). Senates, unions, and the flow of power in American higher
education. *Canadian Journal of Higher Education*, 13(1), 51–64. Retrieved from
http://journals.sfu.ca/cjhe/index.php/cjhe/article/view/182884

Kemerer, F. R., & Baldridge, J. V. (1975). *Unions on campus: A national study of the consequences
of faculty bargaining*. San Francisco, CA: Jossey-Bass.

Kemerer, F. R., & Baldridge, J. V. (1975–1976). The impact of faculty unions on governance.
Change, 7(10), 50–51, 62.

Kemerer, F. R., & Baldridge, J. V. (1976). The impact of collective bargaining on campus
administrators. Retrieved from ERIC database. (ED138126)

Kemerer, F. R., & Baldridge, J. V. (1980). Unions in higher education: The going gets tougher.
Phi Delta Kappan, 61, 714–715.

Kemerer, F. R., & Baldridge, J. V. (1981). Senates and unions: Unexpected peaceful coexistence. *Journal of Higher Education*, 52, 256–264.

Kesselring, R. G. (1991). The economic effects of faculty unions. *Journal of Labor Research*, 12,
61–72.

Kezar, A. (2013). Non-tenure-track faculty's social construction of a supportive work environment. *Teachers College Record*, 115(12). Retrieved from http://www.tcrecord.org ID Number: 17242.

Kezar, A., & Sam. C. (2010). Understanding the new majority of non-tenure-track faculty in
higher education: Demographics, experiences, and plans of action *[ASHE Higher Education
Report*, 36(4)]. San Francisco, CA: Jossey Bass.

Kim, D., Twombly, S., & Wolf-Wendel, L. (2008). Factors predicting community college faculty satisfaction with instructional autonomy. *Community College Review*, 35(13), 159–180.

Klass, B. S., & McClendon, J. A. (1995). Crossing the line: The determinants of picket line
crossing during a faculty strike. *Journal of Labor Research*, 16, 331–346.

Klein, M. W. (2010). Ten years after managed professionals: Who owns intellectual
property now? *Journal of Collective Bargaining in the Academy*, 2. Retrieved from
http://thekeep.eiu.edu/jcba/vol2/iss1/2/

Krause, M., Nolan, M., Palm, M., & Ross, A. (Eds.). (2008). *The university against itself: The
NYU strike and the future of the academic workplace*. Philadelphia, PA: Temple University
Press.

Krieg, J. M., Wassell, C. S., Jr., Hedrick, D. W., & Henson, S. E. (2013). Collective bargaining
and faculty job satisfaction. *Industrial Relations*, 52, 619–644.

Kugler, I. (1997). The 1966 strike at St. John's University, a memoir. *Labor's Heritage, 9*(2), 4–19.

Ladd, E. C., Jr., & Lipset, S. M. (1973). *Professors, unions, and American higher education.* Berkeley, CA: Carnegie Foundation for the Advancement of Teaching.

Ladd, E. C., Jr., & Lipset, S. M. (1975). *The divided academy: Professors and their politics.* New York, NY: McGraw-Hill.

Ladd, E. C., Jr., & Lipset, S. M. (1978). *Technical report 1977 survey of the American professoriate.* Storrs, CT: Social Science Data Center, University of Connecticut. (ED167000)

Lang, S. (1981). *The file: Case study in correction (1977–79).* New York, NY: Springer-Verlag.

Lawler, J. J. (1982). Faculty unionism in higher education: The public sector experience. *Labor Law Journal, 33,* 475–480.

Lawler, J. J., & Walker, J. M. (1979). Dual unions and political processes in organizations. *Industrial Relations, 13,* 32–43.

Lawler, J. J., & Walker, J. M. (1980). Interaction of efficacy, commitment, and expectations in the formation of faculty attitudes toward collective bargaining. *Research in Higher Education, 13,* 99–114.

Lee, B. A. (1978). Collective bargaining in four-year colleges: Impact on institutional practices *[AAHE/ERIC Higher Education Research Report, 7(5)].* Washington, DC: American Association for Higher Education.

Lee, B. A. (1979). Governance at unionized four-year colleges: Effect on decision-making structures. *Journal of Higher Education, 50,* 565–585.

Lee, B. (1982). Contractually protected governance systems at unionized colleges. *Review of Higher Education, 5,* 69–85.

Lee, J. J., Osegura, L., Kim, K. A., Fann, A., Davis, T. M., & Rhoads, R. A. (2004). Tangles in the tapestry: Cultural barriers to graduate student unionization. *Journal of Higher Education, 75,* 340–361.

Leslie, D. W. (1975). Conflict and collective bargaining *[AAHE-ERIC Higher Education Research Report, 4(9)]. Washington, DC: American Association of Higher Education.*

Leslie, D. W., & Ikenberry, D. J. (1979). Collective bargaining and part-time faculty: Contract content. *Journal of the College and University Personnel Association, 30*(1), 18–26.

Leslie, L. L., & Hu, T.-W. (1977). The financial implications of collective bargaining. *Journal of Education Finance, 3,* 32–53.

Lester, J. A. (1968). *The American Federation of Teachers in higher education: A history of union organization of faculty members in colleges and universities, 1916–1966* (Unpublished doctoral dissertation). University of Toledo, Ohio.

Liao-Troth, M. (2008). Correlates of faculty unionization voting behavior. *Journal of Collective Negotiations, 32,* 305–315.

Lillydahl, J. H., & Singell, L. D. (1993). Job satisfaction, salaries, and unions: The determination of university faculty compensation. *Economics of Education Review, 12,* 233–243.

Lindeman, L. W. (1975). Institutional goals and faculty attitudes toward collective negotiations. *Research in Higher Education, 3,* 205–215.

Linville, J. E., Antony, J. S., & Hayden, R. A. (2011a). The collective good: Unionization, perceived control, and overall job satisfaction among community college faculty. *Community College Journal of Research and Practice, 35,* 359–382.

Linville, J. E., Antony, J. S., & Hayden, R. A. (2011b). Unionization and perceived control among community college faculty. *Community College Journal of Research and Practice, 35,* 330–351.

Longmate, J. (2010). The overload debate: How Olympic College leveled the field, sort of.... *Community College Journal, 12*(1), 12, 7.

Love, K. G., Speer, A., & Buschlen, E. (2015). The impact of university culture on unionized faculty intention to strike. *Journal for Higher Education Management, 30*(1), 34–50.

Lozier, G. G. (1977). Negotiating retrenchment provisions. In G. W. Angell, E. P. Kelley, Jr., & Associates, *Handbook of faculty bargaining* (pp. 232–257). San Francisco, CA: Jossey-Bass.

Lozier, G. G., & Mortimer, K. P. (1974a). *Anatomy of a collective bargaining election in Pennsylvania's state-owned colleges.* University Park, PA: Pennsylvania State University, Center for the Study of Higher Education. Retrieved from ERIC database. (ED091981)

Lozier, G. G., & Mortimer, K. P. (1974b). *Faculty voting behavior in the collective bargaining elections for the Pennsylvania State Colleges and University System and Temple University.* Retrieved from ERIC database. (ED089596)

Lozier, G. G., & Mortimer, K. P. (1976). A collective bargaining election: Issues and faculty voting behavior. *Research in Higher Education, 4,* 193–208.

Lyne, B. (2011). Campus clout, statewide strength: Improving shared governance through unionization. *AAUP Journal of Academic Freedom, 2.* Retrieved from: https://www.aaup.org/sites/default/files/Lyne.pdf

Lyons, J. F. (2008). *Teachers and reform: Chicago public education, 1929–1970.* Urbana: University of Illinois Press.

Magney, J. R. (1999). Faculty union organizing on the research campus. *Thought & Action, 15*(1), 111–126.

Maitland, C. (1987). Temporary faculty and collective bargaining in higher education in California. *Journal of Collective Negotiations in the Public Sector, 16,* 233–257.

Maitland, C., & Rhoades, G. (2001). Unions and faculty governance. In H. S. Wechsler (Ed.), *NEA 2001 Almanac of Higher Education* (pp. 27–33). Washington, DC: National Education Association.

Maitland, C., & Rhoades, G. (2005). Bargaining for contingent faculty. In H. S. Wechsler (Ed.), *NEA 2005 Almanac of Higher Education* (pp. 75–81). Washington, DC: National Education Association.

Maitland, C., Rhoades, G., & Smith, M. F. (2009). In M. F. Smith (Ed.), *NEA 2009 Almanac of Higher Education* (pp. 75–84). Washington, DC: National Education Association.

Marshall, J. L. (1979). The effects of collective bargaining on faculty salaries in higher education. *Journal of Higher Education, 50,* 310–322.

May, A. M., Moorhouse, E. A., & Bossard, J. A. (2010). Representation of women faculty at public research universities: Do unions matter? *Industrial and Labor Relations Review, 63,* 699–718.

Mayhall, B. R., Katsinas, S. G., & Bray, N. J. (2015). Thinking about tomorrow: Collective bargaining and labor relations in higher education. *Journal of Collective Bargaining in the Academy, 0*(10), article 8, 1–42. Retrieved from http://thekeep.eiu.edu/jcba/vol0/iss10/8

McClendon, J. A., & Klass, B. (1993). Determinants of strike-related militancy: An analysis of a university faculty strike. *Industrial and Labor Relations Review, 46,* 560–573.

McConnell, T. R. (1971). *The redistribution of power in higher education.* Berkeley: University of California, Center for Research and Development in Higher Education. Retrieved from ERIC database. (ED048842)

McFerron, J. R., Camp, R. C., Lynch, D. M., & Woods, J. L. (1996). Tenure standards within statewide systems of higher education: The collective bargaining milieu. *Journal of Collective Negotiations in the Public Sector, 25,* 365–375.

Meador, M. & Walters, S. J. K. (1994). Unions and productivity: Evidence from academe. *Journal of Labor Research, 15,* 373–386.

Megel, C. (1956, October). Collective bargaining v. collective begging. *American Teacher, 41,* 11–12.

Metchick, R. H., & Singh, P. (2004) *Yeshiva* and faculty unionization in higher education. *Labor Studies Journal, 28*(4), 45–65.

Monks, J. (2000). Unionization and faculty salaries: New evidence from the 1990s. *Journal of Labor Research, 21,* 305–314,

Moore, J. W. (1971). *Pennsylvania community college faculty: Attitudes toward collective negotiations.* University Park, PA: Pennsylvania State University, Center for the Study of Higher Education. Retrieved from ERIC database. (ED051801)

Morand, M. J., & McPherson, D. S. (1980). Unionism's effect on faculty pay: Handicapping the available data. *Monthly Labor Review, 103*(6), 34–36.

Morgan, D. R., & Kearney, R. C. (1977). Collective bargaining and faculty compensation: A comparative analysis. *Sociology of Education, 50,* 28–39.

Moriarty, J., & Savarese, M. (2006). *Directory of faculty contracts and bargaining agents in institutions of higher education.* New York, NY: National Center for the Study of Collective Bargaining and the Professions, Hunter College of the City of New York.

Mortimer, K. P. (1974). Research data on tenure and governance under collective bargaining. Retrieved from ERIC database. (ED100200)

Mortimer, K. P., & Lozier, G. G. (1972). *Collective bargaining: Implications for governance.* University Park, PA: Pennsylvania State University, Center for the Study of Higher Education. Retrieved from ERIC database. (ED067059)

Mortimer, K. P., & Lozier, G. G. (1973). Contracts of four-year institutions. In E. D. Duryea & R. S. Fisk (Eds.), *Faculty unions and collective bargaining* (pp. 108–129). San Francisco, CA: Jossey-Bass. (ED067059)

Mortimer, K. P. & Richardson, R. C., Jr. (1977). *Governance in institutions with faculty unions: Six case studies.* University Park, PA: Pennsylvania State University, Center for the Study of Higher Education. Retrieved from ERIC database. (ED140764)

Muczyk, J. P., Hise, R. T., & Gannon, M. J. (1975). Faculty attitudes and the election of a bargaining agent in the Pennsylvania State College System—II. *Journal of Collective Negotiations in the Public Sector, 4,* 175–188.

Murphy, M. (1990). *Blackboard unions: The AFT & NEA, 1900–1980.* Ithaca, NY: Cornell University Press.

Myers, C. B. (2011). Union status and faculty job satisfaction: Contemporary evidence from the 2004 National Study of Postsecondary Faculty. *Review of Higher Education, 34,* 657–684.

Nagowski, M. P. (2006). Associate professor turnover at America's public and private institutions of higher education. *American Economist, 50*(1), 69–79.

Nasstrom, R. R. (1986). A contractual no-layoff guarantee in higher education. *Journal of Collective Negotiations in the Public Sector, 15,* 357–365.

National Labor Relations Board v. Yeshiva University, 444 U.S. 672 (1980).

Nelson, C. (Ed.). (1997). *Will teach for food: Academic labor in crisis.* Minneapolis: University of Minnesota Press.

Nelson, C. (2011). What faculty unions do. Retrieved from https://www.jamesgmartin.center/2011/03/what-faculty-unions-do/

Neumann, Y. (1979). Determinants of faculty attitudes toward collective bargaining in university graduate departments: An organizational climate approach. *Research in Higher Education, 10,* 123–138.

Neumann, Y. (1980). Organizational climate and faculty attitudes toward collective bargaining: A university in a major labor dispute. *Research in Higher Education, 13,* 353–369.

Newcomer, J., & Stephens, E. C. (1982). A survey of patterns of unit composition at public higher education institutions involved in collective bargaining. *Journal of Collective Negotiations in the Public Sector, 11,* 89–111.

Newfield, C. (2008). *Unmaking the public university: The forty-year assault on the middle class.* Cambridge, MA: Harvard University Press.

Newton, D. (1973). CUNY—A grievous situation. In J. P. Begin (Ed.) *Academics at the bargaining table: Early experience* (pp. 62–68). New Brunswick, NJ: Rutgers University, Institute of Management and Labor Relations. Retrieved from ERIC database. (ED082701)

Nixon, H. L., II. (1973). Factoring a faculty's attitudes. *Change, 5*(2), 10–11, 61.

Nixon, H. L., II. (1975). Faculty support of traditional labor tactics on campus. *Sociology of Education, 48,* 276–286.

Odewahn, C. A., & Spritzer, A. D. (1976). Administrators' attitudes toward faculty unionism. *Industrial Relations, 15,* 206–215.

O'Meara, K., Terosky, A. L., & Neumann, A. (2008). Faculty career and work lives: A professional growth perspective *[ASHE Higher Education Report, 34(3)].* San Francisco, CA: Jossey-Bass.

Ormsby, J. G., & Ormsby, S. Y. (1988). The effect of unionization on faculty job satisfaction: A longitudinal study. *Journal of Collective Negotiations in the Public Sector, 17,* 153–160.

Ormsby, J. G., & Watts, L. R. (1989). The effect of unionization on organizational commitment: A longitudinal study of a university faculty. *Journal of Collective Negotiations in the Public Sector, 18,* 327–336.

Ormsby, J. G., & Watts, L. R. (1991). College faculty unionization and its effect on the gender/job satisfaction relationship. *Journal of Collective Negotiations in the Public Sector, 20,* 43–52.

Orze, J. J. (1975). Faculty collective bargaining and academic decision making *[Special Report No. 24].* Washington, DC: Academic Collective Bargaining Information Service. Retrieved from ERIC database. (ED116571)

Patel, V. (2016, August 26). A new era for grad-student organizing. *Chronicle of Higher Education.* Retrieved from http://www.chronicle.com/article/A-New-Era-for-Grad-Student/237572

Perna, L. W. (2001). Sex and race differences in faculty tenure and promotion. *Research in Higher Education, 42,* 541–567.

Perna, L. W. (2003). The status of women and minorities among community college faculty. *Research in Higher Education, 44,* 205–240.

Porter, S. R. (2013). The causal effects of faculty unions on institutional decision-making. *Industrial and Labor Relations Review, 66,* 1192–1211.

Prial, F. J. (1987, February 26). District 65 becomes unit of the U.A.W. *New York Times.* Retrieved from http://www.nytimes.com/1987/02/26/nyregion/district-65-becomes-unit-of-the-uaw.html

Rassuli, A. L. I., Karim, A., & Roy, R. A. J. (1999). The effect of experience on faculty attitudes toward collective bargaining: A cross-temporal analysis. *Journal of Labor Research, 20,* 203–218.

Rees, D. I. (1993). The effect of unionization on faculty salaries and compensation: Estimates from the 1980s. *Journal of Labor Research, 14,* 399–422.

Rees, D. I. (1994). Does unionization increase faculty retention? *Industrial Relations, 33,* 297–321.

Rhoades, G. (1993). Retrenchment clauses in faculty union contracts: Faculty rights and administrative discretion. *Journal of Higher Education, 64,* 312–347.

Rhoades, G. (1996). Reorganizing the faculty workforce for flexibility: Part-time professional labor. *Journal of Higher Education, 67,* 626–659.

Rhoades, G. (1998). *Managed professionals: Unionized faculty and restructuring academic labor.* Albany: State University of New York Press.

Rhoades, G. (1999). Medieval or modern status in the postindustrial university: Beyond binaries for graduate students. *Workplace, 2*(2). Retrieved from http://louisville.edu/journal/workplace/issue4/rhoades.html

Rhoades, G. (2013). Bargaining quality in part-time faculty working conditions: Beyond just-in-time employment and just-at-will non-renewal. *Journal of Collective Bargaining in the Academy, 4.* Retrieved from http://thekeep.eiu.edu/jcba/vol4/iss1/

Rhoades, G., & Rhoads, R. A. (2003). The public discourse of U.S. graduate employee unions: Social movement identities, ideologies, and strategies. *Review of Higher Education, 26,* 163–186.

Rhoades, G., & Torres-Olave, B. M. (2015). Academic capitalism and (secondary) academic labor markets: Negotiating a new academy and research agenda. In M. B. Paulsen (Ed.) *Higher education: Handbook of theory and research* (Vol. 30, pp. 383–430). New York, NY: Springer.

Rhoads, R. A., & Rhoades, G. (2005). Graduate employee unionization as symbol of and challenge to the corporatization of U.S. research universities. *Journal of Higher Education, 76,* 243–275.

Richardson, R. C., Jr., & Riccio, E. (1980). Collective bargaining and faculty involvement in governance. *Community College Review, 7*(3), 60–65.

Riesman, D. (1973). Commentary and epilogue. In D. Riesman & V. A. Stadtman (Eds.), *Academic transformation* (pp. 409–474). New York, NY: McGraw-Hill.

Rogers, S. E., Eaton, A. E., & Voos, P. B. (2013). Effects of unionization on graduate student employees: Faculty-student relations, academic freedom, and pay. *Industrial and Labor Relations Review, 66,* 487–510.

Rothgeb, J., & Mitakides, K. (2015). Academic unions in recessionary times. *Journal of Economics and Politics, 22*(1), Article 1. Retrieved from http://collected.jcu.edu/jep/vol22/iss1/1

Rothman, S., Kelly-Woessner, A., & Woessner, M. (2011). *The still divided academy: How competing visions of power, politics, and diversity complicate the mission of higher education.* Lanham, MD: Rowman & Littlefield.

Rubin, B. M., & Rubin, R. S. (2007). Graduate student employees and their propensity to unionize: Part II, the Illinois experience. *Journal of Collective Negotiations, 31,* 241–249.

Ruiz, E. A. (2007). The stone that struck Goliath: The part-time faculty association, Washington State Community and Technical Colleges, and class-action lawsuit. In R. L. Wagoner (Ed.), *New Directions for Community Colleges: No. 140. The current landscape and changing perspectives of part-time faculty* (pp. 49–54). San Francisco, CA: Jossey-Bass.

Saltzman, G. M. (2000). Union organizing and the law: Part-time faculty and graduate teaching assistants. In H. S. Wechsler (Ed.), *NEA 2000 Almanac of Higher Education* (pp. 43–55). Washington, DC: National Education Association. Retrieved from http://www.nea.org/assets/img/PubAlmanac/ALM_00_05.pdf

Saltzman, G. M. (2012). An anti-union tide: The 2011 attack on public employees' bargaining rights. In M. F. Smith (Ed.), *NEA 2012 Almanac of Higher Education* (pp. 35–46). Washington, DC: National Education Association. Retrieved from http://www.nea.org/assets/docs/_2012_Almanac_Saltzman_final.pdf

Sanders, J. (1979). *Cold war on the campus: Academic freedom at the University of Washington,* 1946–64. Seattle: University of Washington Press.

Schenk, T. (2010, January 17). The effects of graduate-student unionization on stipends (Working Paper Series 1831975*).* Cambridge, MA: National Bureau of Economic Research. Retrieved from http://tomschenkjr.net/wordpress/wp-content/uploads/2009/07/eegsu.pdf

Schmid, J. (2001). Forces of separation and solidarity: Building and sustain a graduate employee union at the University of Iowa–Part two. *Journal of the Midwest Modern Language Association, 34*(3), 8–13.

Schmidt, P. (2014a, February 26). AAUP leaders face backlash over unionization emphasis. *Chronicle of Higher Education.* Retrieved from http://www.chronicle.com/article/AAUP-Leaders-Face-Backlash/144985/

Schmidt, P. (2014b, April 18). AAUP officers win elections that focused on their union emphasis. *Chronicle of Higher Education.* Retrieved from http://www.chronicle.com/article/AAUP-Officers-Win-Elections/146057

Schmidt, P. (2016, July 25). How much can unions lift adjuncts? CUNY contract fight hinges on what's good enough. *Chronicle of Higher Education.* Retrieved from http://chronicle.com/article/How-Much-Can-Unions-Lift/237238

Schneider, A. (1997, March 7). Graduate student on 30 campuses rally for unions, better pay. *Chronicle of Higher Education.* Retrieved from http://www.chronicle.com/article/Graduate-Students-on-30/76081

Schuster, J. H., & Finkelstein, M. J. (2006). *The American faculty: The restructuring of academic work and careers.* Baltimore: Johns Hopkins University Press.

Scimecca, J., & Damiano, R. (1967). *Crisis at St. John's: Strike and revolution on the Catholic campus.* New York, NY: Random House.

Scott, J. (2000). The struggle for union justice and social justice at the University of Iowa. *New Labor Forum, 6,* 108–115.

Seidman, J., Edge, A., & Kelley, L. (1974). Attitudes of Hawaiian higher education faculty toward unionism and collective bargaining. *Journal of Collective Negotiations in the Public Sector, 3,* 91–119.

Seidman, J., Kelley, L., & Edge, A. (1974a). Faculty bargaining comes to Hawaii. *Industrial Relations, 13*, 5–22.

Seidman, J., Kelley, L., & Edge, A. (1974b). Faculty views of faculty senate and university administration in Hawaiian higher education. *Journal of Collective Negotiations in the Public Sector, 3*, 373–387.

Sherman, F. E., & Loeffler, D. (1971). Universities, unions, and the rule of law: The teaching assistants at Wisconsin. *Wisconsin Law Review, 229*, 187–209.

Simson, G. (1975). Solidarity never! The professoriate and unionization at the University of Hawaii. *Journal of Collective Negotiations in the Public Sector, 4*, 267–296.

Singh, P., Zinni, D. M., & MacLennan, A. F. (2006). Graduate student unions in the United States. *Journal of Labor Research, 27*, 55–73.

Slaughter, S. (1993). Retrenchment in the 1980s: The politics of prestige and gender. *Journal of Higher Education, 64*, 250–282.

Smith, C. (2003). Working systemically to improve the conditions of part-time/adjunct faculty: A case study of the Washington Federation of Teachers' public and legislative campaign. *WorkingUSA, 6*(4), 23–31.

Smith, T. L. (1992). The impact of university faculty unionization on the male-female wage differential. *Journal of Collective Negotiations, 21*, 101–110.

Smith, T. L., & Grosso, J. L. (2009, October). *The union influence on the male-female wage differential: Evidence from public universities.* Paper presented at the Global Conference on Business & Economics, Cambridge University, UK.

Sosin, K., Rives, J., & West, J. (1998). Unions and gender pay equity in academe: A study of U.S. institutions. *Feminist Economics, 4*(2), 25–45.

Sproul, C. R., Bucklew, N., & Houghton, J. D. (2014). Academic collective bargaining: Patterns and trends. *Journal of Collective Bargaining in the Academy, 6*(1), 5. Retrieved from http://thekeep.eiu.edu/jcba/vol6/iss1/5

Staller, J. M. (1975, April). Collective bargaining: Its effect on faculty at two-year public colleges. In T. M. Mannix (Ed.), *Collective bargaining in higher education. Proceedings, third annual conference* (pp. 74–87). New York, NY: National Center for the Study of Collective Bargaining in Higher Education.

Stubaus, K. R. (2015). The professionalization of non-tenure track faculty in the United States: Three case studies from public research institutions: Rutgers, The State University of New Jersey, University of Illinois at Urbana-Champaign, and University of Oregon. *Journal of Collective Bargaining in the Academy, 0*(34). Retrieved from http://thekeep.eiu.edu/jcba/vol0/iss10/34

Sullivan, R. (2003). Pyrrhic victory at UC Santa Barbara: The struggle for labors new identity. In D. M. Herman & J. M. Schmid (Eds.), *Cogs in the classroom factory: The changing identity of academic labor* (pp. 91–116). Westport, CT: Praeger.

Swofford, J. (1984). Part-time faculty and the appropriate bargaining union in two-year colleges. *Journal of Collective Negotiations in the Public Sector, 13*, 67–84.

Thomas, S. L., & McGehee, V. (1994). Faculty bargaining in private colleges: Beyond Yeshiva. *Employee Responsibilities and Rights Journal, 7*, 297–315.

Thompson, K. (1994, May). *Central contingencies: Part-time faculty and the future of higher education.* Paper presented at Academic Unionism and Part-time Faculty: Strategies for Change, New York.

Thompson, J. (2003). Unfinished chapters: Institutional alliances and changing identities in a graduate employee union. In D. M. Herman & J. M. Schmid (Eds.), *Cogs in the classroom factory: The changing identity of academic labor* (pp. 118–135). Westport, CT: Praeger.

Trottman, M., & Belkin, D. (2016, July 17). Labor board ruling could allow grad students to unionize. *Wall Street Journal.* Retrieved from http://www.wsj.com

Turner, V. B. (1919). The American Federation of Teachers. *Monthly Labor Review, 9*(2), 247–255.

Twombly, S., & Townsend, B. K. (2008). Community college faculty: What we know and need to know. *Community College Review, 36*(1), 5–24.

U.S. Bureau of Labor Statistics (2016). *Union members—2015* [USDL-16-0158]. Retrieved from http://www.bls.gov/news.release/pdf/union2.pdf

Van Ells, M. D. (1999). More than a union: The Teaching Assistants Association and its 1970 strike against the University of Wisconsin. *Michigan Historical Review, 25*(1), 103–124.

Van Sell, M. P., Barclay, L. A., Willoughby, F. G., & York, K. M. (2006). Faculty satisfaction with unions: The impact of personal instrumentality and active commitment. *Journal of Collective Negotiations, 31*, 33–44.

Walker, J. M., & Lawler, J. J. (1982). University administrators and faculty bargaining. *Research in Higher Education, 16*, 353–372.

Walker, J. M., & Lawler, J. J. (1986). Union campaign activities and voter preferences. *Journal of Labor Research, 7*, 19–40.

Walters, D. E. (1973). Collective bargaining in higher education: Its impact on campus life and faculty governance. In J. P. Begin (Ed.), *Academics at the bargaining table: Early experience* (pp. 16–24). New Brunswick, NJ: Rutgers University, Institute of Management and Labor Relations. Retrieved from ERIC database. (ED082701)

Wassell, C. S., Jr., Hedrick, D. W., Henson, S. E., & Krieg, J. M. (2015). Wage distribution impacts of higher education faculty unionization. *Journal of Collective Bargaining in the Academy, 7*. Retrieved from http://thekeep.eiu.edu/jcba/vol7/iss1/4

Weed, C. F. (1987). Faculty collective bargaining after a decade in public and private colleges in New Hampshire. *Journal of Collective Negotiations in the Public Sector, 16*, 265–293.

Weingarten, R. (2016, August 23). AFT President Randi Weingarten on NLRB ruling in Columbia Case. Retrieved from http://www.aft.org/press-release/aft-president-randi-weingarten-nlrb-ruling-columbia

White, M. D. (1982). The intra-unit wage structure and unions: A median voter model. *Industrial and Labor Relations Review, 35*, 565–577.

Wickens, C. M. (2008). The organizational impact of university labor unions. *Higher Education, 56*, 545–564.

Wiley, C. (1993). A historical look at the effect of collective bargaining on faculty salaries in California community colleges. *Journal of Collective Negotiations in the Public Sector, 22*, 157–172.

Williams, G. B. (1989). Collective bargaining – A change in the locus of control at two-year colleges. *Journal of Collective Negotiations in the Public Sector, 18*, 253–272.

Williams, G. B., & Zirkel, A. P. (1988). Academic penetration in faculty collective bargaining contracts in higher education. *Research in Higher Education, 28*, 76–92.

Williams, O. B., & Zirkel, P. A. (1989). Shift in collective bargaining issues in higher education: A review of the literature. *Journal of Collective Negotiations in the Public Sector, 18*, 73–88.

Wilson, B. J., III, Holley, W. H., & Martin, J. S. (1983). Effects of faculty unions on administrators' attitudes toward issues in higher education. *Journal of Collective Negotiations in the Public Sector, 12*, 231–242.

Wollett, D. (1974). Faculty collective bargaining in higher education: An organization perspective. *Journal of Law and Education, 3*, 427–437.

Wurth, J. (2016, May 29). Here are provisions of new 5-year contract with non-tenure-track faculty at UI. *The News-Gazette.* Retrieved from http://www.news-gazette.com/news/local/2016-05-28/here-are-provisions-new-5-year-contract-nontenure-track-faculty-ui.html

Zabel, G. (2000). A new campus rebellion: Organizing Boston's contingent faculty. *New Labor Forum, 6*, 90–98.

Zalesney, M. D. (1985). Comparison of economic and noneconomic factors in predicting faculty vote preference in a union representation election. *Journal of Applied Psychology, 70*, 243–256.

Zamudio-Suaréz, F. (2016, August 4). CUNY union ratifies contract to provide raises and multiyear contracts. *Chronicle of Higher Education.* Retrieved from http://chronicle.com/blogs/ticker/cuny-union-ratifies-contract-to-provide-pay-raises-multiyear-contracts/113355

Zhou, Y., & Volkwein, J. F. (2004). Examining the influences on faculty departure intentions: A comparison of tenured versus nontenured faculty at research universities using NSOPF-99. *Research in Higher Education, 45*, 139–176.

Zorn, S. (1971). Unions on campus. In P. G. Altbach, R. S. Laufer, & S. McVey (Eds.), *Academic super markets* (pp. 288–302). San Francisco, CA: Jossey Bass.

Name Index

A

Adler, D. L., 90
Alexander, P., 49
Ali, S. M., 53
Alleman, N. F., 13
Allen, R. E., 51
Ambash, J. W., 121
Andes, J., 81, 83, 89, 91
Antony, J. S., 94, 99
Arnold, G. B., 23, 98
Ashraf, J., 69, 70, 71, 72, 74
Aussieker, B., 65, 123
Aydin, R., 71

B

Bacharach, S. B., 68
Bain, T., 73, 88
Baker, H. K., 67, 74
Baldridge, J. V., 42, 45, 77, 80, 82, 83, 86, 89, 90, 95, 96, 108, 109, 141
Baldwin, R. G., 107
Balkin, D., 77, 78
Balkin, D. B., 77
Barba, W. C., 124, 127
Barbezat, D. A., 69, 70, 74
Barclay, L. A., 99
Bauer, S. C., 68
Bayer, A. E., 43, 44
Beauvais, L. L., 103
Begin, J. P., 49, 73, 82, 89, 96
Beisse, F., 123

Belkin, D., 16
Benedict, M. E., 72, 84
Benjamin, E., 33
Berman, M., 51
Bernhardt, R. G., 49
Berry, J., 17, 36, 37, 38, 40, 41, 107, 112, 119
Beveridge, M. D., 78
Bigoness, W. J., 49, 52
Birnbaum, R., 63, 64, 66, 96, 97, 98, 102
Blader, S., 126
Blandin, J., 49
Blixt, S. L., 53
Bognanno, M. F., 75
Bornheimer, D. G., 52
Borstoff, P. C., 53
Bossard, J. A., 84
Boyd, W. B., 132, 133
Bray, N. J., 72, 73
Breitzer, S. R., 124
Brewer, A. M., 53
Brickell, J., 91
Broad, M. C., 121
Browne, M. J., 69
Brown, W. R., 85, 87
Brown, W. W., 65, 66, 68, 74, 77, 82
Brumbaugh, R. B., 47
Bucklew, N., 18, 94
Budke, J. M., 113
Buschlen, E., 58

Goodwin, H. I., 81, 109
Gordon, M. E., 99
Graf, L. A., 54
Greenberg, I., 117
Gress, J. R., 49, 50
Gross, A., 124
Grosso, J. L., 76
Gumport, P. J., 126, 128
Guthrie-Morse, B., 67, 72, 74, 82

H

Haehn, J. O., 46
Hagengruber, D. L., 48
Halesah, O., 102
Hammer, T. H., 51
Hansen, W. L., 75
Hardesty, C., 56
Harris-Pereles, K. L., 103
Haviland, D., 13
Hayden, G. M., 122
Hayden, R. A., 94, 99
Hedgepeth, R. C., 77, 81, 89, 95
Hedrick, D. W., 71, 72, 74, 76, 78, 79, 134
Hemmasi, M., 54
Henson, S. E., 71, 72, 74, 76, 78, 134
Herbert, W. A., 17
Herman, D. M., 124
Herziger, W. A., 31
Hess, J., 112
Hewitt, G. J., 127, 128
Hicks, S., 73
Hill, M. D., 77, 97, 99
Hines, E., 91
Hise, R. T., 47
Hobgood, W. P., 97
Hoeller, K., 114, 117
Hoffman, E., 112
Holley, W. H., 83, 96
Holsinger, N., 57, 58
Houghton, J. D., 18, 94
Hurd, R., 34, 35
Hutchens, M. B., 20
Hutchens, N. H., 20
Hutcheson, P. A., 20
Hu, T. W., 66, 67, 72, 74

I

Ikenberry, D. J., 109, 110, 111
Ingerman, S., 123
Inman, D., 96, 98, 102
Ito, H., 66, 68

J

Jackson, P. I., 68
Jacobs, J. A., 99
Jaeger, A. J., 107
Johnson, B., 124
Johnson, K. Q., 124
Johnson, M. D., 85
Johnstone, R. L., 18, 32, 75, 81, 85, 91, 92
Julius, D., 85, 86, 93
Julius, D. J., 23, 36, 83, 93, 126, 128

K

Kammeyer-Mueller, J. D., 57
Karim, A., 54
Karim, A. R., 53
Katchanovski, I., 59
Kater, S., 93
Kathawala, Y., 78, 83, 99
Katsinas, S. G., 72, 73, 79
Kazlow, C., 48
Kearney, R. C., 65, 66, 67
Kearns, A., 126
Keaveny, T. J., 51
Kelley, L., 46, 47, 95
Kelly-Woessner, A., 59
Kemerer, F. R., 42, 45, 77, 80, 82, 86, 89, 90, 95, 96, 109
Kesselring, R. G., 68
Kezar, A., 23, 107, 116
Kezsbom, A. T., 129
Kim, D., 99
Kim, K. A., 20, 126, 128, 131
Klaff, D. B., 129
Klass, B., 55
Klass, B. S., 55
Klein, M. W., 92
Krall, L., 75
Krause, M., 35, 124
Krieg, J. M., 71, 72, 76, 78, 79, 100, 101
Kugler, I., 18, 31

Subject Index

A
American Association of University
Professors (AAUP), 8, 18
American Council on Education, 43, 121
American Federation of Government
Employees (AFGE), 38
American Federation of Labor's (AFL), 27
American Federation of Teachers (AFT), 8,
18
Art Institute of Philadelphia, 41
Association of American Colleges (AAC),
28

B
Bryant College of Business Administration,
18

C
California Faculty Association, 113
California State Colleges, 46
California State University and Colleges
(CSUC), 50
California State University System, 39
Carnegie Commission on Higher
Education, 22, 43
Carnegie Council National Survey of
Higher Education, 70
Central Michigan University, 51
Chronicle of Higher Education, 129
City Colleges of Chicago, 41

City University of New York (CUNY), 16,
63
Coalition of Contingent Academic Labor,
108
Coalition on the Academic Workforce
(CAW), 115
Cogs in the Academic Faculty, 124
Collective bargaining in higher education
(CBHE), 35
College and University Personnel
Association (CUPA), 82
Communication Workers of America
(CWA), 38
Communist Party, 29
Congress of Industrial Organizations
(CIO), 29
Contractual language, 87
Cost of living (COL), 65

D
Depression-era AFT campus, 119
The Divided Academy, 58

F
First Red Scare, 27
Fisk University, 30
Free Speech Movement, 123

G
Gender wage gap, 76
General Information Survey, 69

Graduate student unionization:
background and setting, 119–122;
research on, 122–130
Grapevine, 73
Great Depression, 107

H

Howard University, 29

I

Indiana University, 126
Integrated Postsecondary Education Data
System, 76

K

K–12 education, 39

L

Local 1021, 16

M

Milwaukee State Normal School, 27
Milwaukee State Teachers College, 27

N

National Center for Education Statistics's
(NCES), 37
National Center for the Study of Collective
Bargaining in Higher Education and the
Profession's (NCSCBHEP), 17
National Council for Higher Education,
40
National Education Association (NEA), 8,
18, 53
National Labor Relations Board (NLRB),
16
National Study of Postsecondary Faculty
(NSOPF), 70
Nazi Germany, 29
New York College Teachers Union, 29
The New York Times, 121
New York University (NYU), 35
Non-tenure-line and part-time faculty
unionization, 106–107; background and
setting, 107–108; research on, 108–
117

North American Academic Study Survey
(NAASS), 58

P

Pennsylvania State College system, 47
Popular Front, 29
Principal investigators (PI), 113

R

Rutgers University, 96, 113, 120

S

Service Employees International Union's
(SEIU), 9, 16
Soviet Union, 29
Stanford Project on Academic Governance,
45
Statement on Academic Freedom and
Tenure, 83
*1940 Statement on Academic Freedom and
Tenure,* 28
State University of New York (SUNY), 41,
63
State University System of Minnesota, 86

T

Tallahassee Community College, 16
Teaching Assistants Association's (TAA),
122
Temple University, 48
Tenure-line faculty, attitudes and voting
behaviors of, 42–43, 60–61; attitudes
and attributes, 43–50; economic and
noneconomic factors, 50–53; lessened
attention in the 21st century, 56–59;
small-scale studies, 53–56
Tenure-line faculty unions, effects of,
61–62; collegiality and campus
relationships, 95–98; compensation,
62–80; faculty unionization, 101–103;
governance and faculty influence,
88–95; satisfaction, 98–101; tenure,
grievance procedures, and retrenchment
policies, 80–88
Tri-State College, 30
Tufts University, 120

About the Author

Timothy Reese Cain is an associate professor in the Institute of Higher Education at the University of Georgia. He has degrees from Duke University (AB), The Ohio State University (MA), and the University of Michigan (PhD); from 2005–2013 he was a member of the faculty of the University of Illinois at Urbana-Champaign. His work explores historic and modern issues involving academic freedom, unionization and professionalization, academic administration, student speech rights, and related issues. It raises questions about how U.S. higher education has been organized, staffed, influenced, and controlled, while also pointing to the importance of individual agency and group action in shaping policies and procedures. He is the author of numerous journal articles and book chapters, as well as *Establishing Academic Freedom* (Palgrave Macmillan, 2012) and, with colleagues at the National Institute for Learning Outcomes Assessment, *Using Evidence of Student Learning to Improve Higher Education* (Jossey-Bass, 2015). He is currently writing a book on the history of college faculty unionization.